THE
EMOTION
BEHIND
MONEY

THE EMOTION BEHIND MONEY

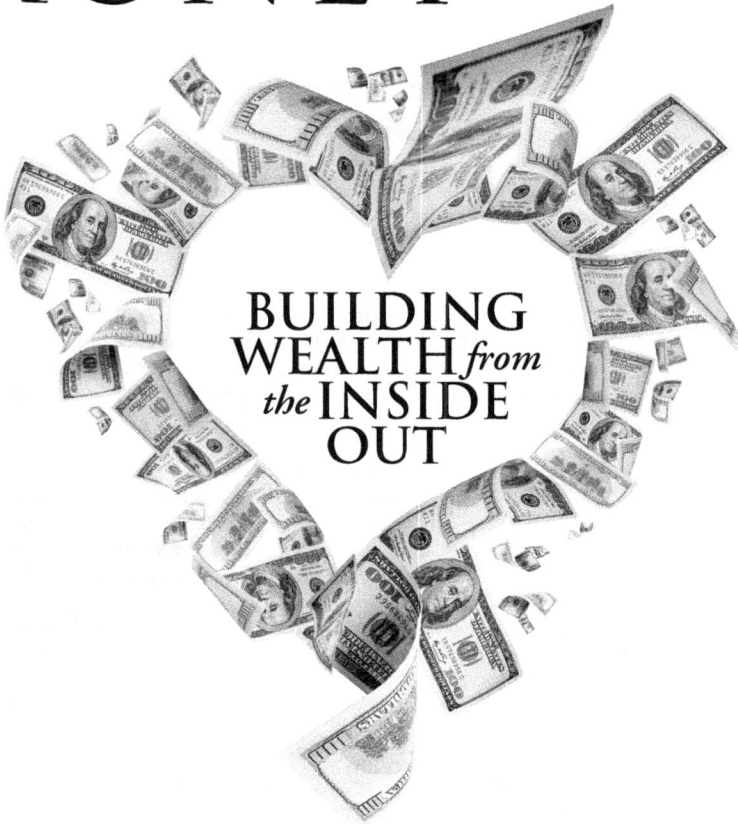

BUILDING WEALTH *from* *the* INSIDE OUT

JULIE MARIE MURPHY, CFP®

Beyond Your Wildest Dreams, LLC

Chicago, Illinois

THE EMOTION BEHIND MONEY:
BUILDING WEALTH FROM THE INSIDE OUT
Julie Murphy, CFP

Copyright © 2020
Beyond Your Wildest Dreams, LLC 1st Edition, 2008

Beyond Your Wildest Dreams, LLC
1017 W. Washington Blvd
Chicago, IL 60607

Library of Congress Control Number 2013937640

ISBN 978-1-935766-79-7

Book design by BYJ Communications, Inc.
Cover design by MACook Design

PLEASE NOTE: The views, comments, and opinions expressed within this writing are solely those of Julie Marie Murphy, not those of any co-workers, managers, broker-dealer staff or management, regulators, or other industry professionals except where specifically cited. The ideas and opinions presented are not meant to fit every individual and in some cases, professional help in the form of medical, tax, and legal advice may be necessary and should be obtained from qualified professionals before attempting to implement serious changes to your life.

The hypothetical illustrations contained herein are intended solely to depict how a Financial Advisor may obtain and implement recommendations suited to an individual or business need. The depictions in these examples have been created from a compilation of clients, are for illustrative purposes only, and do not reflect the actual performance of any particular investment or the analysis of the needs of an actual person or business. For more information about the options available, please contact a qualified professional.

Julie Marie Murphy does not offer tax advice. The tax information contained herein is general and is not exhaustive by nature. It was not intended or written to be used, and it cannot be used by any taxpayer for the purpose of avoiding penalties that may be imposed on the taxpayer under U.S. federal tax laws. Federal and state tax laws are complex and constantly changing. You should always consult your own legal or tax advisor for information concerning your individual situation.

This material is neither an offer to sell nor the solicitation of an offer to buy any security, which can only be made by the prospectus which has been filed or registered with the appropriate state and federal agencies, and sold only by broker/dealers authorized to do so. No regulatory agency has passed on or endorsed the merit of this material. Any representation to the contrary is unlawful. All trademarks referenced herein are the property of their respective owners.

I dedicate this book to my clients, siblings, parents,
aunts, uncles, teachers and mentors:
May your generosity and guidance be returned to you
ten thousand fold!

Affirmations for Wealth Building

I choose to recognize my emotions behind money.

I choose to have my financial choices determined by who I really am in every fiber of my body.

I choose to let my life control my finances instead of allowing my finances to control my life.

I choose to face my current financial reality.

I choose to follow my desired financial roadmap and let that guide me out of my current financial reality.

I choose to position myself to be lucky.

I choose to love myself enough to live a passionate and purposeful life.

I choose a life of financial abundance and inner peace.

emo·tion

noun

a: the affective aspect of consciousness: feeling **b:** a state of feeling **c:** a conscious mental reaction (as anger or fear) **subjectively experienced as strong feeling usually directed toward a specific object** and typically accompanied by physiological and behavioral changes in the body

synonyms see *feeling*

Source: Merriam-Webster's Collegiate Dictionary, 11th Edition

CONTENTS

Acknowledgments   i

About the People in This Book   iii

Introduction   v

Section One: **The Big Picture**   1

Chapter One: Your Inner Wealth   3

Chapter Two: The Search for Happiness   25

Chapter Three: Breaking Away from Inherited Beliefs   47

Section Two: Choose to Change   71

Chapter Four: Own Your Personal Power   73

Chapter Five: Your Turning Point   93

Chapter Six: The Crabs in Your Bucket   111

Chapter Seven: Facing Your Financial Reality   131

Section Three: Financial Transformation   141

Chapter Eight: Setting Your Intentions   143

Chapter Nine: Lives That Thrive   173

Chapter Ten: Building and Renovating Your Portfolio   189

Epilogue   Welcome to the Beginning   201

Appendix 1   Job Function Worksheet   203

Appendix 2   Suggested Reading and Other Resources   205

ACKNOWLEDGMENTS

Mom, thank you for teaching me to write! Dad, thank you for giving me the drive and determination to do anything! Mom and Dad, thank you for the love and support that helped me become who I am today! God Bless!

I would like to thank my siblings: Marianne, Donnie, Brian, Matt, Colleen, Danny, Mark, Timmy, Peter, Johnny and my birthday buddy, Katie. The personal gifts that you've shared throughout the years have enriched and sustained me in countless ways. Thanks for your unconditional love. We are all extensions of each other.

When times were tough, my aunts and uncles came to the rescue! Thank you for taking time out of your lives to show me that there was a different way of being. Thanks also for showing me that anything is possible; you just have to choose it to make it real. I love you all!

I'd like to thank the many mentors who guided me on my journey. Sue Boner, my high school basketball coach, inspired in me the importance of teamwork, mutual respect, integrity and commitment. Thanks to Bob Lyman for taking a chance on me when all the cards were stacked against my succeeding in the financial services business. Bob, I would not be where I am at this moment without your love, support and guidance, for which I'm eternally grateful.

My clients, thank you for trusting my financial guidance as I embarked on this mission to help financially heal the world. If you had not shared your challenges with me, I would not be able to help others as effectively.

To my various friends, current and past staff members and strategic alliances, particularly Candy Mayer, Jennifer Brennan, Jim and Janet VanHuysse, Steve and Stephanie Murphy, Maureen Laschober, Ann Persico, Veli Sanchez, Kelly Farritor, Erin Duncan, Jennifer Lake, Nina Hartigan, Vanessa Sheehan, Justin Lee, Jeff Ragan, Jennifer Medina, Jessica Leshin, Melissa Casserly, Mark Murphy, Tiffany Andreae, David Wells, Deb Murphy, Joe Ziccardi, thank you for spending a part of your life's journey and helping me manifest my dreams and the dreams of those important to me.

To my women's business owner group, the Beyond My Wildest Dream team, thank you for helping me clarify my vision for what my life's purpose is today and helping me to create worldwide financial healing.

I'm extremely gratified to have found these inspirational teachers and guides whose great wisdom and understanding showed me how to help others find the emotion behind money: Caroline Myss, Linda McCabe, Dr. Deepak Chopra, Dr. David Simon, Louise Hay, Marianne Williamson, Brian O'Toole, Dan O'Toole, Rhonda Byrne, Laura Day, Marie-France Collin, Eckhart Tolle, Kathleen Schaffer, Katrina Laflin and Mary Ann Daly.

Last, but not least, I'd love to thank every single person who made this book a physical reality: Karyn Pettigrew, Bob Lyman, Mark Murphy, Melissa Casserly, Sharon Rossmaessler, Crystal Wilson, Martha Porter-Fiszer, Athena Golianis, Chris Deschaine, Bob Rainone, Laura McFarland-Taylor, Gayle Mandel, Judy Katz, Bonnie Egan and Bruce Jacobson. Without each of your individual talents, this would have been a much steeper climb. You're the best!

I love you all so very much!

ABOUT THE PEOPLE IN THIS BOOK

Over the course of my career I've been richly blessed with a colorful mosaic of clients. I am continually amazed at the honesty, depth and integrity of the people I serve, many I've known for more than a decade. We share a mutual trust and commitment to living life to its fullest. As an added bonus, I enjoy their company.

For reasons of privacy, not to mention myriad legalities, the case studies in this book are not based on any real individuals. They are compilations of client histories and experiences, and the names used are fictitious. I'm telling you this for two reasons. First, because I have no choice; it's a requirement of legal compliance. The second reason, however, goes to the heart of this book. It's my hope that by including these relatable stories about people and their money, you will gain a deeper understanding of my unique approach to wealth management. My intent is that by viewing wealth building through the lens of other people's experiences, your eyes will be opened to the possibilities of a new reality for yourself—a reality filled with happiness, prosperity and inner peace.

INTRODUCTION

God bless Suze Orman. Whether you love her or hate her, one thing is for certain: Suze's tough-love approach to money management has invigorated millions of Americans with the concept of financial empowerment.

I have a special place in my heart for the polarizing waitress-turned-financial-guru, and here's why. In an early 2007 interview in *The New York Times Magazine*, Suze disclosed some tidbits about her personal net worth, including how she has it distributed. Her critics were instantly abuzz with judgments about Suze's portfolio, and how it does not align with conventional investment wisdom, let alone with her own advice. One critic even claimed her investments were characteristic of a "retired grandmother with no heirs." So, what's to love about that? Well, I'll tell you. I think Suze is doing what's right for Suze and nobody else, and I believe that's the way it should be, especially when it comes to money.

Not long after I started my firm, in 1995, I discovered something that was never taught in business school. It's the notion that each of us has our own unique and personal relationship with money. It begins even before you get your first piggy bank or receive your first couple of bucks to buy ice cream, and over the years it changes very little. It may evolve ever so slightly as you leave home, join other communities and take on the responsibilities of a respectable tax-paying citizen, but, for the most part, your feelings about money have been imprinted on you practically from birth. Those emotions are responsible for how you make money and how you keep it, or how it seems to go out the door faster than it comes in. Those feelings actually influence how much money you'll make throughout your entire life.

Now I'm going to let you in on a little secret. Unless you're in touch with those emotions and understand the impact that they have on your financial behavior, *and* unless you take steps to change or heal some of those behaviors, you will not achieve the wealth and happiness you desire. It's that simple.

I see this phenomenon manifest all the time in the portfolios of intelligent, hard-working people who have habitually gravitated toward certain types of financial products because of what was going on in their hearts, not in their heads. I have one client, a divorced executive and mother in her early forties, who came to me a few months ago asking for my help with a 401(k) rollover. As we got to talking and I learned what was in her portfolio, I was aghast! This bright, successful, well-meaning single mother was so afraid of not having enough money for her kids if something were to happen to her, that she used life insurance products to meet practically all of her "savings" and far too many of her "retirement" needs. This is a perfect example of someone who let her emotions get in the way of good planning. She was cheating herself of higher returns and lower tax implications because of an inner fear of losing money that directly stemmed from her childhood. In essence, she was perpetuating a life of struggle. I'm not sharing this woman's situation with you to point out her mistakes. I'm offering this as a hypothetical, as I will many others throughout this book, so that you can begin to understand the power that your emotions have over your financial well-being.

Like most people, I always thought that if you had millions, life was better. All troubles ceased and you were livin' on Easy Street. I also always believed that the surest sign of wealth was having lots of stuff, and that having that stuff was the key to happiness. I've since learned that wealthy people are not the ones who have more. In actuality, financially wealthy people have needs and desires no different from those who don't have as much financial wealth; the price tags are simply bigger. Now I see wealth as a state of mind. It involves being rich in every facet of your life, including your work, financial, family, personal and spiritual life.

As a financial professional with a thriving business, I've met many multimillionaires. I now see that their issues are the same as anyone else's; there are just more zeros. I didn't come from money; I had to work for everything I've ever had. I've racked up credit card debt. I've had student loans. I've had lots of money and I've lost or spent lots of money. When it comes to creating a plan for wealth, none of that really matters. What's more important is to understand the "why" *behind* the behavioral swings that occur in your financial life. To find out, you must tap into the many feelings, fears and beliefs bubbling below the surface, deep within your soul.

The bottom line is that wealth doesn't come from managing your money. Wealth comes from managing the *emotions* behind your money.

On the following pages I am going to help you discover financial healing. I'll show you how to get in touch with your subconscious money issues and learn to recognize their presence in your life—from the balance in your checking account to the people you choose to turn to for financial advice. I will also help you create a personal strategy based on you and you alone—a plan that helps you rebuild your emotional foundation as it relates to making financial decisions—all while giving you the steps necessary to achieve a life of infinite possibilities.

I'm also going to ask you to participate in some exercises, so you'll want to have a notebook or pad of paper and a pen or pencil handy.

Does that sound too good to be true? Well, I have thousands of clients and my own life as living proof that your dreams *can* and *will* become your reality. You can achieve happiness and wealth in your portfolio and in your soul. All you need is a little guidance from me and a little inspiration from something that is very near and dear to your heart: your innermost dreams and desires. You've got them—now let's tap into them!

SECTION ONE
The Big Picture

"Our deepest fear is not that we are inadequate. Our deepest fear is that we are powerful beyond measure. It is our Light, not our Darkness, that most frightens us."

—Marianne Williamson

1

YOUR INNER WEALTH

ere's a word I bet you haven't heard many financial professionals use: abundance. You're going to hear it quite a bit from me because my goal is to teach you how to discover and live a life of abundance—financially, personally and professionally. What's even more unusual is that we're going to get there by exploring your emotional and spiritual DNA.

Oh, I know what you're thinking. You thought this was going to be a book about money, not a bunch of touchy-feely stuff. Well, you're partially right. This is a book about making and keeping money while being happy with your life and the path that you have chosen to take. But why would a successful, independent wealth advisor with an MBA give a hoot about emotional health and spirituality? It's because, after more than a decade of teaching clients how to build and hold on to wealth, I've discovered that there are two huge factors that determine financial success. One is how you process your emotions. The second is how you create harmony or balance in your life.

What Is at the Center of Your Life?

Answer this question: What is the most important thing in your life right now? Don't think too hard. Just say whatever pops into your head. Now, hold on to that answer. Write it down if you want to. I bet by the time you've finished reading this chapter your answer will change.

Unless you're a modern-day Rip Van Winkle who's just awakening from a century of sleep, you're probably all too aware that money runs the world today. It's as if we are handcuffed to the Almighty Dollar. Without money, it seems we cannot achieve peace, health or happiness. If you're like most people I've met, there has probably been a time in your adult life when you were so sick of your job that all you wanted to do was march into the corner office and offer up a giant piece of your mind, followed by the words "I quit!" You didn't do it though, did you? That's because many of us have painted ourselves into a corner trying to maintain a certain lifestyle. The fear of losing your job, which means potentially losing your current standard of living, is pretty intense, isn't it? I know how you feel. Been there, but I didn't do that!

One memorable evening some time ago I was at a popular place called Brother Jimmy's in Chicago with my then boyfriend, now ex-husband, Billy. I recall feeling ready to pack my bags and trade my career for a beachcomber's lifestyle in the Caribbean. Soon after that, though, I did some diligent soul-searching, and at the same time found a couple of great mentors who brought me to a new reality. In this new reality, I turned my focus away from money

Figure 1

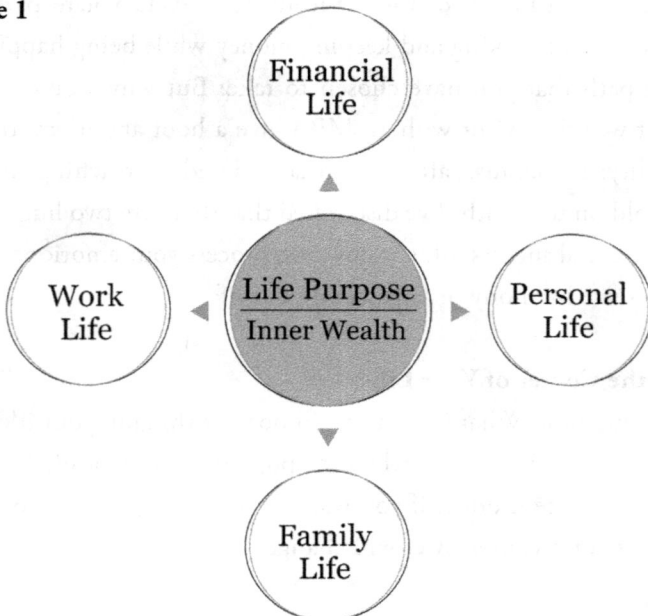

and let my "Inner Wealth" lead the way. Your Inner Wealth is the part of you that contains your conscience, values and core beliefs—all of the nonphysical characteristics that make up your spiritual DNA. It's also the source of your dreams, your desires, your individuality and your life's purpose..

When I put these forces at the center of my existence, allowing all the other parts of my life—from my job to my family to my finances—to balance themselves off that center like the extensions on a hanging mobile, my life changed dramatically!

The Life Navigation Wheel

Because I am a numbers person, a left-brainer, always trying to communicate numbers to creative right-brainers, I've found success using diagrams. They help me grasp more esoteric concepts and bring them to life. I created the Life Navigation Wheel (see Figure 1) as a way to communicate to my clients how most of us prioritize our lives. You may have seen diagrams similar to the one illustrated here. Basically, it consists of five realms:

1. Financial

2. Personal

3. Family

4. Work

5. Spirit (which I refer to as your Life Purpose/Inner Wealth)

At this very moment, one of these realms is at the center of your life. It's the motivation behind practically every decision you make. This is because whatever is at the center of your world creates a powerful force, a *gravity* that keeps all other aspects of your life circling it in an emotional and spiritual orbit.

When I ask new clients to tell me what is at the center of their lives, I typically get a look of panic or angst. I believe this is because deep within us there is a conflict between what we think our life's focus should be and what it actually is. We each have a life that we create, and it's not anyone's place to judge the choices made along the way, including ourselves. Still, the amount of shame, guilt, sadness and regret that surrounds this issue astounds me. After years and years of coaching people through this painful reality, I've observed an interesting connection between age and what is perceived as an acceptable life focus. Most middle-aged married folks believe that family should be the center of their wheel. Twenty- and thirty-something up-and-comers generally say they should be focused on work. Retired folks believe that the personal realm, especially health, should be their main motivation. Without fail, however, every single person I counsel expresses, often tearfully, the same frustration. They aren't living the life they want, and it's all because of the money choices they've made. Unfortunately, this is because most of us in the Western world have come to believe that money is the answer to life's discomforts, and the source of all happiness. It's the magic key to the coveted kingdom of Gotta-Have-It-Can't-Live-Without-It. It has become the central focus of practically every life decision we make (see Figure 2).

What about you? What's at the center of your existence? More importantly, what do you *want* to have at the center of your world?

Figure 2

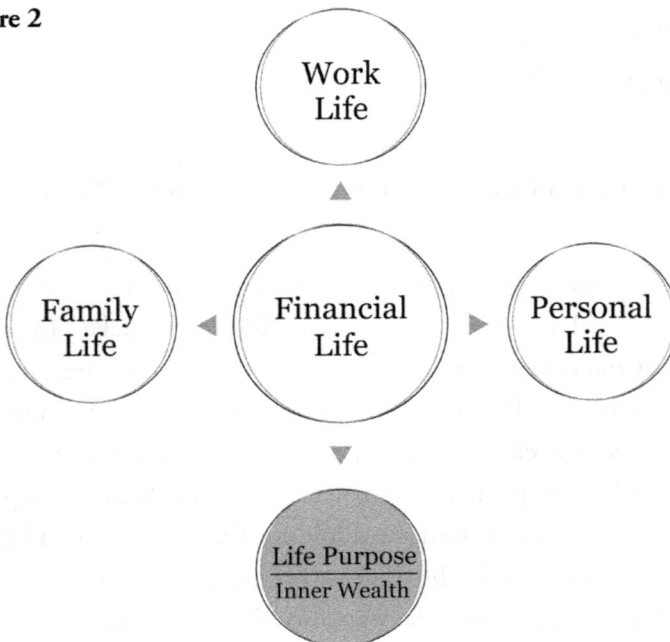

The Power of Money

I hate to be the bearer of bad news, but if you're like I was, or even remotely similar to the thousands of people I've counseled over the years, the center of your life is either financial or work-related. This may not be what you want to hear, but, for most of us, it's true. Without fail, an unhealthy, money-centric life is the most common issue I see, regardless of net worth or age. Of course, this isn't very surprising, is it? In our culture, money really is the center of everything. As Americans we have turned our power over to the Almighty Dollar, so it's not surprising that we all recognize the "almighty" in the idiom. Sadly, this is neither profitable nor healthy. We let our money and/or our lifestyle dictate our lives. It's not difficult to see why. Just look around you. We live in a money-focused society, consuming things from "stuff" to food to experiences right now, at whatever cost. That's what it's all about, right? Stuff, stuff, stuff! I'm not pointing this out to be critical. I just want to open your eyes to a potential reality in which you derive your personal power from your quality of life rather than from the *quantity* of things you own. You have the personal power to change your focus. How? It's by developing a healthier relationship with money and in so doing, creating a greater balance and harmony within yourself. I call this living life from the inside out!

1 EXERCISE

Inner Wealth Exercise

Let's take a minute right now to focus on your Inner Wealth. First, I'd like you to think about all the things that are important to you—your spouse, kids, siblings and parents, your health, your career and job title, hobbies, pets. Make a list. It doesn't have to be in any particular order. Next, think about the values you uphold—peace, honesty, prosperity, beauty, integrity, strength, humility, etc. Write them down. Finally, take note of the beliefs you embrace. Do you have faith in a higher power? Is a sense of community paramount to your existence? Is freedom of speech or self-expression necessary in your world view of peace and prosperity? Try not to feel either self-critical or proud of your answers. Just write them down. Now, read back over your list and consider this: Is it possible that you're living a life that is not consistent with these priorities, values and beliefs? Does this exercise create a sense of guilt or longing within? If the answer is yes, welcome to the human race, my friend. You're not alone. Recognizing the gap is half of the battle. You've begun the financial healing process, so let's get to it!

Your Authentic Self

In order to put your life in alignment and put the true *you* at the center, you must first undergo a shift in your current perceptions and how you focus on the future. As I had to teach myself to do, you must learn to direct your attention away from money and toward the things that you listed in the Inner Wealth exercise. We all have an emotional and spirit-driven infrastructure that guides us through life. This infrastructure is who you are—your authentic self. When you recognize the strength and purpose of that foundation, and allow your dreams and intentions within to guide you, rather than the numbers in your savings or checking account, amazing things begin to happen. It may take you awhile to overcome your resistance to believing this, but it's true. When you know who you are and what you want your life to be, and then put some practical action into the process, you will begin to live your dreams, and the money will follow. When you change your mindset and behavior, your reality will change.

Getting Unstuck?

Are you still holding back? Are you filled with doubt? Many of us have had so many disappointments or perceived failures in our lives that cynicism is only natural. Perhaps you feel totally stuck in a bad place, mentally or emotionally, even physically. If you do, it's easy to understand why. Change is a scary thing. It's easier to stick with what's familiar. I know plenty of people who long for a new focus in their lives, but they're just too settled into the status quo—even though they're feeling trapped in the very life they created—to do anything about it. This is because they're not in touch with what truly makes them happy. They have not been open to their sense of self, or what their authentic self can accomplish.

Have you ever had a time in your life where you were doing something and time flew by because whatever you were doing absolutely excited you? When this happens, it's usually a clear sign that you're following the direction of your Inner Wealth. It's also a sign that you're embracing your special talents, skills or gifts, or as I like to say, your unique ability. Whenever we utilize our own unique abilities, we can't help but feel tickled! When people are not happy about their jobs, marriage or family life, it's usually because they are not being true to who they are. Instead, they give their personal power away to their fears, which then drive their lives. They are not being or doing what they were put on this earth to do. The good news is that everything will begin to fall into place once you have tapped into the emotional and spiritual framework that constitutes *you*. Easier said then done? Not really... stay tuned!

2 EXERCISE

Authentic Self Exercise

Think back to when you were a child. Can you recall doing anything that seemed instinctive to you? Were there activities that engaged you to the point of total absorption? In certain moments did time seem to fly by? What types of activities came naturally to you? Now, bring yourself into the present moment. What do you truly enjoy doing with your time? If money were no object, what would you do with your life every day? What are you truly great at? What is it that no one else in the entire universe can do better than you? Come on, don't be modest. Make a list. Make it a long list. It's all right; no one will judge your list, not even you! Give yourself permission to put it down on paper. I'll bet no one else can even touch your ability to understand your kids. Perhaps you're the king of analysis, able to assess a situation in a nanosecond and then articulate your findings. Who else but you can calmly navigate the chaotic seas of home and work life with the heart rate of a Zen master? Perhaps your gift is to be present in the moment, to "just be." Maybe you're a gifted listener, or you make the best Irish stew from here to Halsted Street, as my grandfather used to say. You get the picture. After you've made your list, look it over. I expect that you'll learn something about yourself that you hadn't really thought of before. Regardless, you're on the road to aligning your life with your authentic self. Isn't this great? Hang on, here we go!

What Defines You on the Outside?

There's a popular story, which has become somewhat of an urban myth, about the man who works hard his entire life to provide for his wife and children and then, just as he claims his pension or Social Security check, he suddenly keels over and dies. How many stories have you heard about people who finally reach retirement and some catastrophe happens—they become gravely ill or a criminal talks them into revealing their bank account number and steals their life's savings? It's because these people have given their personal power away to money. What's more, they've forgotten to continuously redefine their life throughout its different stages. They've lost their sense of purpose. In essence, they are trapped in a single definition of life's meaning. When exterior forces alter that definition, their reason for living is destroyed, and their bodies soon follow.

My father is a good example of this scenario. An electrician in Local Union 134, he began working as an apprentice at the age of seventeen. Like many other unions back in the mid '80s, his trade union functioned on a seniority system, meaning the more senior laborers got the less strenuous jobs, especially as they neared retirement. As luck would have it, just as Dad's life was supposed to be getting easier, they revamped the system to one that made no concessions for age or seniority. Like many of his peers, Dad was in a no-win situation. He suddenly had to compete for work with agile young laborers half his age, and half his cost to the employer. Anyone who has ever been through a corporate restructure knows what this kind of upheaval can do to one's physical, mental and emotional state. This turn of events in my dad's life changed him forever.

With electrical jobs more difficult to get, Dad was out of work much more than in the past. He simply couldn't maintain the same speed and capacity as the younger guys, so he was consistently laid off. On November 8, 2005, Dad received a letter from the union telling him that, because of his lack of work over the past two years, he would no longer receive a subsidy from the union to pay for his living expenses. That day Dad suffered two massive strokes. The first was while driving home from work and the other while he was already in the hospital. They rendered him paralyzed for six months, and he is still recovering today. When my brother Mark went to clean out Dad's totaled car, he found the letter from the union cutting him off. My family was shocked and absolutely infuriated! How could a guy who put his time in, working extremely hard all his life to raise twelve children, be tossed away like an old pair of shoes? The sad truth is that these things happen far too often, and unless you structure your life so you're insulated from hardships like these, your mental, emotional or physical health will suffer. Even your relationships with others will become damaged. The signs of these consequences are everywhere—cancer, obesity, failing marriages, the enormous amounts of anti-anxiety medications being taken—these are all the result of lives driven by work, money and lifestyle choices.

Giving Your Personal Power Away to Money

My office is not far from a Metra train station in downtown Chicago. On my drive to work each morning, I see hundreds of men and women step off the train wearing expressions of pure drudgery. They look like they've been punched in the face. They hit the pavement, heads hanging down, all sour and sad-looking. Clearly, they are not having fun, or even *remotely* enjoying their work lives. Take a look around for yourself and you'll see.

Today when I see these people, I am extremely grateful for the financial healing and harmony I experienced in my life. I used to feel like those folks getting off the Northwest Train Line at 7:55 a.m. I felt like everything I did, day in and day out, 24/7, had to do with money commitments. Back in 1995, as a new insurance and investment broker, I was bummed and tired every morning of the week, because, in my mind, money was the hub of my life. I was stuck in the middle of the forest and couldn't get through the trees to see the clearing. Talk about the rat race! I never seemed to have enough money. I needed enough for groceries and to pay the rent on my modest apartment. I needed enough to go out with friends, especially because I typically picked up the tab (for emotional reasons I'll explain later). I had to sell more insurance and investment products each week to make enough to sustain my youthful spending habits and, Lord knows, I also had to keep enough on hand so that I could help out my eleven siblings (yes, eleven) from time to time. Money was at the center of my life's focus, and I was exhausted! Just like those sad-looking people getting off the train, I had given all my personal power to money. As a result, I was not living in harmony with my inner desires and emotions. My life was out of balance and needed to be healed. Can you relate?

Always on Edge

My most beloved mentor, a man named Bob Lyman, was instrumental in my healing process with money. When I first worked with him, I was a subordinate employee, an agent at a large financial services firm, and Bob was my General Agent. Bob taught me many things about life and money. Because I am a person who wears her heart on her sleeve, when something is bothering me, I don't hide it well; it's written all over my face. Whenever Bob would see me with a look that resembled those folks getting off the train, he would call me into his office, close the door and say, "Okay, Murph, what's up?" I was usually so tied up in knots I'd break down in tears of frustration. Anyone who knows me would tell you that tears are not my style, but back then my inner turmoil was far too intense to contain.

At the time, I was not able to pay my student loans, and this had me in knots. I was barely paying my rent, my siblings needed financial assistance, and I was really sick and tired of eating macaroni and cheese for dinner. I'll never forget when, during one of my more tearful moments, Bob remarked jokingly that my student loans were like a pimple on an elephant's ass. I remember looking at him like he was nuts! Later, however, the brilliance of his comment became a source of inspiration and utter joy for me. It helped me keep it all in perspective. From that day forward, he'd often say, "Hey, Murph, how's that pimple?" It always made me smile and reflect more calmly on my perceived troubles. Maybe things are only as bad as we choose to make them, and perhaps there is more to life than work and money, I considered. What Bob showed me, most of all is that no matter where your current reality is, there are always options. These are the thoughts that put me on the road to my financial healing.

Family Reality

As I said, I grew up with eleven brothers and sisters (yes, I'm Irish, and yes, I'm Catholic). While that didn't help me become a wealth advisor, it sure as heck helped to make me the type of wealth advisor I am. I learned to deal with different personalities because I was forced to. It made me sensitive to others' needs. Growing up the second oldest out of a dozen kids in Midlothian, Illinois, a working class suburb of Chicago, also provided me with quite a bit of emotional baggage in terms of money. Needless to say, healing those emotions has kept me quite busy as an adult—especially considering my career choice!

I had a job from the time I could walk and talk, and that job was to look after my younger brothers and sisters. I can also remember doing homework by candlelight because it was more important to keep the gas on for the heat in the winter months. Also, every time one of us had our First Communion, my parents would borrow all of our gift money to help with the household expenses. To this day, my dad has a book that lists every dime he owes each child. Not that any of us expect to ever see that money!

I got my first paying job, delivering a local paper called the "Penny Saver," when I was six. Wow, I thought I'd won the lottery when I got that first check. It was my first step toward getting the heck out of poverty. That's when I started (dimly, of course—I was still a kid) to realize that money is what gives you choices in life. Before that, I really didn't think there were choices. My mom always said, "Sometimes you just have to make do with what you have," and we always did. We could make things stretch. I remember our Christmas gifts every year were to take old oatmeal containers and decorate them. We'd fill them up with the cookies we baked for all of our aunts and uncles. Those were true Christmas gifts from the heart. Still, I wanted the choice of living a different life.

Every year, my mom would come home with another baby. The bottom ten children were born in twelve years. I can remember getting up in the middle of the night to feed the baby of the house because Mom and Dad were absolutely past the point of exhaustion. Many mornings I would wake up sitting in the recliner with the baby on my chest, and then have to help get all of my other siblings up and out for school.

Birth of a Salesperson

We all went to a Catholic grammar school, and we each had to work off part of our tuition. By 7th grade, I not only delivered the Penny Saver, I also delivered the *Chicago Tribune* and *Chicago Sun-Times* before school and on the weekends. This was a huge pay raise. It was great! I also really got into selling stuff for fundraisers at school. One year I sold merchandise from a "sales kit" that had everything from wrapping paper to oven mitts. This is when it first occurred to me that sales came easily to me and I was really good at it. I was certainly a "people person." I figured out a way to get the things I wanted. It was really easy. All I had to do was what came naturally to me—talk. Interaction, talking and connecting with people were my gifts, and I soon learned that those things made it easy for me to sell. It didn't even seem like work. All through grammar school, my homeroom classmates loved it whenever there was a sales contest for taffy apples because I always sold the most, and our homeroom would win a pizza party. For thirteen years straight, I was the top candy salesperson for the Midlothian girls' softball league fundraiser. But no matter how much money I made, it always got spent fast—nothing went into any kind of savings, not even a piggy bank. Hmm, was there emotion behind the money even then? Definitely!

3 EXERCISE

Getting What You Want Exercise

We all have behaviors that get us things in life. Some are healthy and enable us to accomplish our goals with ease, or at least without negative consequences. There are other patterns of behavior, however, that are less constructive. They may get you what you want in the short term, but in the long run they wreak havoc on your relationships with others, or worse, with yourself. Be honest. Do you frequently play the victim in an attempt to gain someone's sympathy, which in turn forces them to let you have your way? Are you creative, able to brainstorm a variety of means to an end? Do you rush into situations in a panic for fear of losing out to others in the end?

Take a few minutes right now to explore your patterns with me. Write them down as they come to you. I'd like you to think about a recent success, achievement or acquisition. How did you get it? What energy did you expend in the process? For example, let's say you just purchased a new car. What steps did you take to attain it? What emotions or behaviors did you employ to engage with the others involved? Did you first choose to give yourself an amount you could afford, or did you decide to sweet-talk your spouse to get the funds? Did you call up another dealership to see how they would compete? If you did, what was your demeanor with the salesperson—charming, businesslike or demanding? Did you research which car was right for you first, then base your planned cash outflow on that particular car loan? Did you drive all over town for a week to find the ideal car, or did the whole transaction occur in ten minutes?

If you haven't already done so, get a pad and paper and think of a similar incident. Write down the actual steps you took, along with the feelings and behaviors that accompanied them. When you're done, read over your narrative. Can you see yourself following one or more of these behaviors to get what you want in life? Are they healthy behaviors or harmful ones? Don't judge, just ask! What are your habitual patterns? Nobody is going to say anything is good or bad, right or wrong. It's just something for you to recognize and think about without judgment.

My Inherited Money Pattern

Even as a child I found it easy to work with people. I felt comfortable dealing with people, it was natural. This was my first glimpse of using my unique ability. It was fun for me and I enjoyed it. I will never forget the year I won the Atari 2600 game. I was ecstatic. The next year I won a nifty electric blue ten-speed Huffy bicycle. The year after that the Midlo girls softball league just called and asked me what I wanted. I said $100, and that's what I got! Ask and you shall receive...what a concept! With all of that success, by the time I entered high school I still had no money saved. I had spent it all, or given it to the family to keep the house afloat. Now I see that my spending habits were a product of fear—fear that if I didn't buy what I wanted right then and there, I wouldn't have the money later to buy it. This is because all I had known in my life thus far was lack, a life of perpetual struggle, being in survival mode, if you will. I definitely had a scarcity mentality. I was following my parent's money pattern. Before you ever got it, it was already spent. In fact, deep down, I now know that having an abundance of money made me feel uncomfortable. I learned how to create an abundance of money, but I just couldn't abundantly hold onto it.

This pattern was not only how I handled money; it was also how I handled food. I was shocked when I realized how this pattern had leaked out into other areas of my life. It was subtle, but potent. When we were kids, one of my jobs was to go shopping for groceries with Mom once a week. If we had a little more money than usual that month, she would buy a snack for our lunches. That happened about once every couple of months. My personal favorite was Scooter Pies. They were the least expensive, ninety-nine cents for a box of twelve chocolate goodies, and my siblings and I loved them. When mom and I would get home, all of the other kids would charge over to the groceries because they knew when money was good, we'd get Scooter Pies. Mom would let us either eat one right away or decide to save one for our lunches later in the week. We learned quickly that we had to devour our ration immediately, because the treats would be gone long before we even packed our lunchboxes.

A few years ago one of my aunts recalled that it was always really hard when my family showed up for the holidays. It seems we all charged the line to get food, and put way too much on our plates, for fear, I would imagine, of not getting any. On another holiday thirty years later, with all twelve of us now adults, I found I couldn't stop thinking about what my aunt told me. Conscious of this reality, when dinner was served, I chose to observe and I couldn't believe my eyes. All my siblings charged for the table. I wouldn't have believed it if I hadn't seen it with my own eyes. It wasn't wrong; it was just how we had learned to behave at a very early age. Scarcity at its finest!

A Constant Sense of Uneasiness

I'd be willing to bet all the money in the world that there is something about money that makes *you* feel uneasy. Maybe it's as simple as feeling that money runs every decision you make, and you're tired of it—or tired of those gnawing feelings that something is not right, but you can't quite put your finger on what that is. Whenever I get one of those pesky feelings, I stop and take a moment to find out what my body is trying to tell me, because it's a sure sign that something is not aligned between my Life's Purpose and my actions, that is, my inner world versus my external world. Uneasy feelings come when your life is not in harmony with your soul's purpose. Those gnawing feelings usually mean that the life you're living is not in sync with the real you. It's the language spoken by your subconscious in an effort to communicate with your conscious mind. For most of us, this bothersome state of inner turmoil manifests as worry, fear, anxiety, anger, etc.

Now it's time for you to get in touch with some of your own uneasy feelings. While you were reading what I wrote above, did any uneasy feelings come up for you? When you think about money, what nagging thoughts worry you? What gives you a queasy feeling in the pit of your stomach? Make a quick list. I think you'll find that you're not alone.

The most common gnawing, uneasy feelings I hear about money are:

"I never seem to have enough money."

"I can't seem to get out of debt."

"I hate my job, but I'm afraid to quit."

"Why can't I be wealthy and do what I love?"

"How am I going to live the lifestyle I want and still pay the bills?"

"How do I transition from my current reality to my desired life?"

"I have pretty much everything I need, but I want something more, and I don't know what that something more is."

Just as you take care of your body when it feels ill, I want you to learn to take care of your financial health. In order to do that, you must come to understand what those feelings of dissatisfaction or despair mean and where they come from. Feelings are neither right nor wrong; they just are.

We all get gut feelings. Some people believe it's their intuition speaking, or God, the Universe, their dharma, the Holy Spirit, their soul or their conscience. We don't need to get hung up on semantics. It doesn't matter how you define your instincts. What's important is that you learn to recognize when something doesn't feel right. All too often, however, we just go about our lives because that seems to be the path of least resistance. What I've come to realize is that if you're not listening to the messages that you're getting from within, they will keep coming at you, with increasing severity year after year, like an emotional 2x4 that keeps cracking you over the head until you truly listen. Ouch! Why do we do this to ourselves? Life is not supposed to be a constant struggle. Still, it amazes me that so many people have chosen a life of struggle as their constant reality. Sadly, most people wait until they become sick or traumatized before embracing change. We don't have to wait; we can change at any point in our lives. It's our choice! Which route will you choose?

A Toxic Shock

A few times a year I'd treat myself to a week at The Chopra Center for Wellbeing in Carlsbad, California. I find the seminars uplifting, healing and motivating. On my last visit, co-founder David Simon, M.D., mentioned something that shook me to the core. He said that he estimates, based on the patients they see at The Chopra Center, that over 90% of the toxins in the human body are not byproducts of bacteria or harmful chemicals; they develop from toxic emotions. This statement was in alignment with recent insights from a financial perspective, and I had just begun working on this book, so I was eager to speak with Dr. Simon about it. After his seminar I rushed up front and introduced myself. As we talked, he explained how, on a quantum level, we as humans aren't predominantly sick from the toxic foods we eat. We're sick from toxic emotions that are not effectively processed. Wow, talk about an eye-opening moment! I was beginning to see that everything in life is tied to our emotions, from our health to our wealth.

Internal Processing Department

We live in a world so fast-paced that it sometimes seems that we are all trying to catch up with ourselves. Years ago, people used to lean on their communities. Their neighbors, friends or religious congregation helped ease some of life's difficulties. People took more time to care about each other. Seniors retired from companies they had begun working for when they were 18 years old. They were homegrown. Today the face of business is constantly changing. Young employees are coming and going in and out of companies every few years, and the older workers are going out. Who has the chance to get to know anyone anymore?

I don't believe for a minute that we don't *want* to share intimacy. In fact, most people I meet today are starving for someone to care about them on a deeper level. That, I believe, is why so many people look for quick fixes to make themselves feel better, causing a host of problems, like broken homes, consumer debt, obesity and a dependency on prescription drugs. To some degree, we're all trying to process toxic feelings and emotions. However, most of us don't have the psychological infrastructure to process them effectively. Consequently, those emotional toxins show up in our bodies, in our relationships and, overall, in the way we live our lives, making the problem that much worse.

Let me show you how true this also is with respect to your financial health. If you're up to your eyeballs in debt or mortgaged to the hilt, you're in those situations because of your emotions about money and how you internally process those emotions, which then becomes your external reality. It's important for you to know that the feelings and attitudes that you have toward money are neither good nor bad. They are neutral—benign, if you will. It's how you choose to react to those emotions that can either catapult you into financial duress or put you on the positive path to financial abundance.

Here's the best part of all of this: If you can muster up the courage to get in touch with your emotions, you can prevent them from showing up as unhealthy behavior. We'll get into what are unhealthy financial behaviors later. For now, I want you to learn how to recognize your inner toxins in their various forms, from frustration to fear to jealousy, and the like.

4 EXERCISE

Toxic Emotions Exercise

So what exactly is eating you? Spend some time pondering the toxic emotions that you may not be effectively processing. At work, do you consistently break out in a cold sweat at the weekly sales meeting, because you don't like the pressure of performing? Does the health of your mother or father weigh heavily on your mind, leaving you feeling helpless and/or guilty because they live so far away? When you think about next month's mortgage payment, is your stomach in knots? Are your spouse's spending habits a continual source of irritation for you, especially because you keep those thoughts to yourself? How do you choose to respond to your spouse when it comes to money, reactively or proactively? Do you see any patterns in your marriage that seem to come from your parents' relationship with each other and with money? Do you find yourself jealous and angry every time your neighbor mentions her new kitchen, so much so that you avoid talking to her? Open up your heart and let it flow.

Now, here's some good news. There are things you can do to reduce the toxicity of those feelings. The first is allowing yourself to feel these emotions instead of burying them deep inside. Techniques to heal the mind and body include meditation, choosing to create and follow a life plan, revisiting your current life plan if you already have one, or even doing something as simple as redirecting your cash flow, which we will get to in due time.

Stop, Look and Listen

Getting in touch with your toxic emotions is actually as easy as the children's rule for crossing the street: Stop, look and listen. Let's say you wake up Monday morning feeling a little blue. You have to have a cup of coffee (or a Diet Pepsi as I used to) just to muster up enough energy to get out of your pajamas, and then a second cup to get into the car. As you start your forty-minute commute to work, you begin to feel agitated. The radio is on full blast, playing something loud and head-banging, and suddenly you're flipping off drivers left and right. Guess what? Your mind and your body aren't just talking to you—they're screaming! This is an example of how we either have an emotional outburst or bury our emotions in our bodies by numbing ourselves with eating, drinking, smoking, excessive cleaning or exercising, and yes, even spending or hoarding our money. In my past, I can recall that after spending so much on other people for Christmas, I physically experienced what I call a "spending hangover." It was exhausting! Finally I began to actually pay attention to the reasons I overspent. I began to stop, look and listen to what was really going on emotionally that led to my external behaviors.

Humor me and try this. Instead of gulping down all that caffeine, stop and ask yourself, "Why am I so dog-tired and in need of a temporary jolt?" There must be something deep inside you that doesn't want to face the day. Or perhaps you're not sleeping well because all you can think about is the kids' soccer schedules or next week's quarterly meeting. When you get in the car to drive to work, look at your hands on the steering wheel or your eyes in the rearview mirror. Are your knuckles white from clenching or are your eyes narrowed in ire? While you're on the road, instead of blasting the tunes, turn off the radio for a moment and listen to the silence. Your body and mind will start to calm enough to let the "real stuff" going on come to the surface. Try to shut out the busy chatter in your head and focus on your emotions. Or just focus on the silence and allow your emotions to emerge. Think about how you're feeling in the moment. In fact, why not try to listen to your heart this very minute. How are you feeling right now? Get in touch with the sadness or frustration inside that shows itself as anger, rage, jealousy or envy—whatever feelings come up. No judging, just recognize. This kind of exercise is not hard to do, and it's a helpful way throughout the day, to begin to understand your behavior.

The Journey to Abundance

Every day I help smart, well-intentioned people like you take the first steps toward building wealth. First, you must look inside to examine your emotions with regard to money. Then you will need to take steps to get and keep that relationship healthy and strong. It all begins with identifying your own deep-down desires, your life's passions, and allowing them to drive the bus. Finally, you need to map out a Personal Life Navigation route. This is your plan for achieving a life of happiness and abundance. Ultimately, it will be how you choose to navigate your way from your current patterns to a richer foundation in all aspects of your life. Remember the Life Navigation Wheel that I talked about earlier? Your Life Navigation Route is the plan that can shift you from surviving to thriving. It's how you'll progress from a money-centric existence to a life balanced around who you are at your core. By the end of this book, you will have begun to create your own route to pure happiness. You'll be on your way to living your ideal life—not the life of your parents, spouse, friends, neighbors or children—the life *you* want to live.

A Journey from the Inside Out

The journey to financial healing began for me when I decided to look in my own backyard, and this is where you also need to start. If you're a person who already sees your current reality for what it is, then congratulations, because this initial step won't be a problem for you. If, however, you're someone who desperately avoids looking in your own mirror, then you may be somewhat uncomfortable with the process at first. I promise you, though, that once you start asking yourself the right questions and discover who you really are, flaws and all, you will be in a position to live a balanced life, one aligned with your soul's purpose. The payoff will be incredible.

CHAPTER WRAP-UP

Everyone has an Inner Wealth. It's the part of you that contains your conscience, core values, personal dreams and desires. This is who you are, your authentic self.

When you put your Inner Wealth at the center of your life and let it direct your every decision, you can then live a more harmonic life. Your personal, work, family and financial lives will gain purpose and strength from your core.

Western society makes it difficult to listen to your inner compass because it barrages us with messages of external pleasure and excess. This creates an unhealthy relationship with money by fostering the belief that money is responsible for happiness.

You cannot live a life of true happiness and abundance until your relationship with money is healed.

Financial healing is a three-step process. It begins by unplugging from the outside world and focusing inside on your authentic self—your core values, beliefs, unique abilities and sense of purpose. The next step is to define your own personal dreams and desires, to determine what you're passionate about, which is necessary to get what you really want out of life. Finally, you must devise a Personal Navigation Route. This is the life plan that will get you from where you are to where you want to be.

If you know who you are and what you want your life to be, and put practical action into it, the money will follow.

"Follow your Bliss and doors will open where there were no doors before."

—Joseph Campbell

THE SEARCH FOR HAPPINESS

Now that we've established that this wealth-building process begins with you, let's take a peek into the lives of somebody else—the Joneses—that fictitious family that everyone is trying to keep up with. Whenever I bring them up in my seminars, I get a lot of head bobs and nods. We all know who they are in the metaphorical sense, but why do they have so much power?

Actually "Keeping up with the Joneses" was the name of a comic strip that began running in 1913. The Joneses were neighbors of the cartoon's main characters. They were always spoken about but never seen and, just like the Joneses of today, they always seemed to have something "better." I'll bet there were Joneses back in caveman times too. They were those folks next door who displayed all the trendy new and improved stuff, and everyone wanted to have just as much as they had. Ugh.

How We Measure Up

As Americans in the 21st Century, we carry around huge measuring sticks with us wherever we go and use them to size up how we're doing in comparison with each other. This is because Western culture teaches us that wealth is measured from the outside, that it's how much we have that brings happiness. This concept is reinforced everywhere you turn, from your TV screen and the movie screen to the pages of your favorite magazines. The trouble is that this search is inexhaustible, no matter how many zeros you have in your net worth. Whether you're making forty grand a year or half a million, it's nearly impossible to avoid the hamster wheel of life, living paycheck to paycheck, nose to the grindstone, trying to keep up with a certain lifestyle. And this lifestyle, I might add, isn't even based on reality, or on your current cash inflow. The commercials on TV that say drive this car and you'll be like the handsome metrosexual behind the wheel sure don't take into account that you have three kids to put through college. Nor does the ad in the magazine that says invest in our IRA and you'll be like the tanned, perfectly fabulous couple sitting by the pool on their lovely multimillion-dollar estate. Our culture sets the standard for an acceptable life—big house, expensive car, latest fashions and stick-figure bodies. Newsflash everyone: Size zero isn't reality. To me, the "Dove Girls" are. No study has ever proved that money buys happiness.

Survival Mode

After I graduated from the University of Illinois at Urbana-Champaign, I decided to combine my finance degree with my sales talent. After interviewing with forty different companies, I landed a position at an international financial services firm. They had a program where you were considered a "subordinate employee," which meant that they gave you benefits, but no permanent income, and you were responsible for all your expenses. This program allowed me to build my own client base and trained me to become a wealth advisor. At the time I thought that was great.

Looking back, I realize I had taken a job that re-created the financial struggles I had experienced growing up. Most of my college friends were making salaries of $35,000 a year. I was making an advance of $300 per week, which stopped after six months, and I had to pay that back as I sold products. So there I was, $33,000 in debt from student loans, a $23,000 car loan, $8,000 in credit card debt, and I had a job with no secure income. When I made a good sale, I would blow the cash pretty quickly to either catch up on bills or just go out and have a good time with friends to let off steam. I began to realize that if I didn't change how I was operating, I would always be in this cycle of struggling to earn what my lifestyle required. I call this "survival mode." It's doing whatever you can to get by in your current circumstances. Needless to say, this constant struggle for survival is extremely stressful. I also came to the rather sad realization that most people I knew operated like this all of their lives. At the very least, they seemed to go in and out of survival mode. Just because you have a good income, you may think that you're thriving. But you're not really thriving, no matter how much money you make or how much wealth you've built until you're actually living the quality of life that you want to live. As the saying goes, no one ever says on their deathbed, "Wow, I wish I had worked more." Think about it.

A Perpetual Cycle

We've created a lifestyle of constant spending and taking very little personal financial responsibility. Bankruptcies are through the roof, credit card debt is outrageous, and people are taking out second and third mortgages on their homes to pay off this past debt, which means their homes will never be paid off. This explains why, as Robert Kiyosaki says in his book *Rich Dad, Poor Dad* (Business Plus, 2000) there are so many more people today who are income affluent rather than asset affluent. I couldn't agree more.

Our savings rate in the United States has been negative for quite some time. According to a study by the U.S. Department of Commerce, it was negative 1% in 2006—meaning that the average person had saved absolutely nothing and was even somewhat in debt. That's the lowest savings rate since the Great Depression. Let me say that again. In 2006, people saved as little money as during the Depression in the 1930s! We have so much more abundance in our world; yet we save less money. It's those darn Joneses. I don't believe that this is because people don't want to save and accumulate wealth. I think they just don't know how. Many of us are in a self-perpetuating cycle. We were never taught in school how to handle money in abundance. So now it's all about survival.

Here's a quick snapshot of how the cycle feeds on itself. Members of "The Greatest Generation," as Tom Brokaw aptly named them, lived through World War II. They learned how to hold onto a nickel. Many of them never spoke about their finances in front of the children. Instead, money issues were addressed behind closed doors, the "hush-hush" way of communicating. Consequently, the challenge for them soon became, how do you teach a generation about the value of money when that generation of kids never lived through wartime, or even had an open platform to discuss money? Their children, the baby boomers, lived with frugality in their younger years because their parents always saved for the rainy day. Now that the boomers are in their peak income earning years, they are the best spenders in history, and many of them are not prepared for their own retirement. This has created a sense of entitlement within the following generations, "X" and "Y." Since their boomer parents have given them so much, they consciously or subconsciously feel they deserve a life of excess. This year's college graduates will look at money and affluence differently than their parents did when they entered the workforce.

A Financial Generation Gap

I often hear members of older generations say that they are bothered by the carefree spending habits of today's youth. Young people today are good spenders, I will say that. But those of us over thirty-five have an important lesson to learn from our younger peers. They have no fear of failure. Consequently, their minds are open to the concept of abundance. In fact, to some degree they are already living it. Many of them just haven't learned the practice of personal accountability. Instead, they call upon their parents to rescue them from credit hell. And, of course, mom and dad are there to bail them out. It's only natural. Unfortunately, this cycle doesn't help our young people learn to hold on to wealth, a skill necessary for a thriving financial life.

There are obvious financial patterns within every generation. None are right or wrong, good or bad, and it's not our place to judge one another. There are clearly lessons to be learned from every perspective. Each generation has so much to offer. Each has unique gifts that can help make the world become a better place. I believe that mutual respect and understanding of each other's strengths are the hallmarks of a strong, sound community. This is what we all must strive for to achieve global financial stability as well.

The Convenience Factor

Here's another big social influence on your money: convenience. Today we've gotten very comfortable with convenience. I'm certainly a big believer in it, but one of the side effects is that we are less conscious of where our money is flowing. There is something energetically different about swiping a credit card through a machine for a purchase than handing over the same amount in cash. It's as if there is no accountability for that purchase when using a credit card. When clients are having a challenge with cash flow, I encourage them to take a couple of months and use cash for every purchase. The result is amazing. Their spending levels go down significantly, usually somewhere around 10%-30%. According to my professional experience, only one out of every 250 people can successfully manage their cash flow and still use credit cards for regular purchases with full awareness of what they are spending.

Before you think I'm totally ragging on this great country of ours and our spending habits, let me just say there's an upside to our buying behavior. From 2000 to 2002, when the bottom fell out of the market, one of the main reasons it was not a more devastating time for us, I believe, was because of the American consumer. Sure, we were buying all kinds of stuff that we didn't absolutely have to have, but in fact that's what saved us from total ruin: good old consumer spending at its finest. Ironically, the very machine that continually spits out money and then eats it actually saved us! However, I wouldn't count on that always happening.

It's Going to Catch Up With Us

Our cultural fixation with living the good life has also perpetuated a false security about retirement. It's the notion that "I'm going to chic restaurants, hanging with the right crowd, driving the ultimate car, but I'm financially okay because I have a 401(k), to which I contribute just up to my company match. And I'll be able to live this way for as long as I like." Where this thinking falls apart is that if you don't continue to increase your savings as your lifestyle increases, at some point in your life you will have to shrink your lifestyle if you ever plan on retiring. I'm sorry if this sounds harsh, but sooner or later that lifestyle *is* going to catch up with you. These days, just having a retirement plan with your employer is not enough. Although retirement plan balances often seem large, once you adjust for inflation and longevity, it's typically not enough. Unless you began contributing to one very early in life, you will probably come up short at normal retirement age. For one thing, different employers have different limits for maximum contribution. Also, Uncle Sam has a cap on how many pre-tax dollars you can contribute annually. Consequently, the average couple with a household income over $75,000 a year, who start retirement savings later than age thirty, is going to need more than what those limits allow if they want to maintain a comparable lifestyle when they stop working.

As a nation, we also have to wake up to some new realities. Without proper planning, you can't live excessively forever. Let's say you like potato chips. You know you shouldn't eat them all the time so you just eat them once a day. But you eat them once a day, day after day, year after year. Eventually you're going to create health issues, and you'll probably have to go on cholesterol medication because of all that greasy fat you've been ingesting. The same is true of our false sense of financial success. All this over-spending is going to catch up with us in the macro sense via an unhealthy country with an unhealthy economy. In the micro sense, it will bite you in the derriere personally via insurmountable debt or an inability to pay for such necessities as a new roof or braces for the kids. Even worse, you may find yourself living on crackers and Cheez Whiz in your eighties. These are all certainties unless we stop giving our personal power away to money.

We have to stop thinking that happiness can be found through acquisition and start looking inward. Otherwise we'll forever be merely surviving. And I believe that you, my friend, deserve much more than that. The choice is up to you!

Buying False Happiness

So, let's dig down and really, truly find out *why* you've chosen to acquire things to make you happy, albeit temporarily. You can't tell me that you bought that tricked out turbo convertible because you're passionate about making the $600 per month payment. I've never met anyone who absolutely loves all of the financial commitments they must face after receiving their paycheck. Actually, most people I meet say that thinking about their cash flow sucks the life out of them! And it's the same regardless of net worth. I know people with incomes of $40,000 per year and people with incomes that exceed a million bucks a year and they all experience the same phenomenon, the same negative energy. Watching your cash fly right out the window is not unlike the feeling of having your candy snatched away when you were a child. One minute you're holding your sweet money and the next it's gone. Waaaaahhhh!

4 EXERCISE

Acquisition Exercise

I invite you to close your eyes and visualize the last time you bought something that brought you satisfaction. In the moment it excited you, and you showed it off to all your friends. A month or two later, when the credit card bills came in, you experienced a spending hangover. You felt sweaty, queasy or sick to your stomach. Bottom line: Once you had to pay for that financial decision, you found yourself stressed or even filled with dread. We've all been there. Now, answer these questions:

✓ *Did you buy this item to make yourself feel happy?*

✓ *Did you buy it because you were tired of doing without and just said, "What the heck, I'm going to do it"?*

✓ *Did you buy this item to appease or make someone else happy?*

✓ *If you bought it to make someone else happy, were you trying to buy their love? (Many parents today feel guilty because they want to spend more time with their kids, but they also both need to work, so they buy them things out of guilt.)*

✓ *Did you buy this item to feel accepted in your community or neighborhood? Why do you want to be accepted by this group? Is this really what you wanted, or is it that you fear that without it you won't fit in?*

✓ *Are you an emotional spender, meaning do you buy when you're happy or sad?*

✓ *Did that purchase bring you closer to your dreams and desires or farther away?*

✓ *Did you make this purchase without really internalizing what impact it would have on you and your household?*

✓ *What emotions did you temporarily numb or satisfy while you made this purchase?*

Buying from the Heart

When you dig down into your heart to answer these questions, you'll probably start to realize that most overspending is emotionally based. It's motivated by underlying issues. It occurs because we are trying to solve a deeper problem. We want relief from inner pain or discomfort, and we're living under the misconception that, with this new acquisition, the unsettling feelings will go away permanently. But they don't, do they?

Okay, so have I totally pulled the wind out of your sails? I certainly hope not. I just want you to know there is another way, and recognizing the reality of your purchasing behavior is the first step. In my opinion, this initial step is the most challenging and, quite frankly, it's exhausting! Learning to recognize when you're buying things to appease internal discomfort isn't easy. But we all do it. If you just wait a few days before making that purchase, and let the emotions subside, you'll be amazed how your desire changes. It's just not the same as time passes. Try it out. You may still end up making that purchase, and that's great, but by then it will not be an impulse buy. It will have become what I call an "intuitive buy," something that truly adds value to your life because it most likely fills a physical need, not an emotional one. Remember this isn't about not getting what you want in the short term; it's about getting exactly what you desire and deserve in every aspect of your life.

If you don't take a step back to recognize the financial chaos you create in your own life, you'll never, ever, be able to realize your dreams and desires. You'll stay in that state of chaos and disappointment. You'll keep re-creating the yearning for something more. You know the saying, "If you do what you've always done, you'll get what you've always gotten." I'm here to say that if you follow your heart and live the life you dream and desire, you will have financial freedom. To do that, you must shift from a state of being reactive to one that is proactive. So how *do* we shift from this sense of financial survival to financial thriving? The answer is that you have to create a paradigm shift and redesign your approach to true happiness. Come on, follow me. Let's have a little fun!

East Meets West

Back in 2004, a dear friend of mine, Stephanie Moletti, kept raving about a book that she'd read, *Anatomy of the Spirit* by Caroline Myss (Three Rivers Press; 1st edition: August 26, 1997). I was just starting to cultivate an interest in Eastern religion and philosophy, and this was the fourth time I'd heard of this book. If there's one thing I've learned, it's that when you recognize the synchronicities of life, things start taking off in the right direction for you. I figured it was more than coincidence that four people in the past few months had mentioned this book, so I popped into the bookstore and picked up a copy. Let me begin by saying that Caroline Myss is not only a fabulous author, but also a talented medical intuitive. About fifty pages into the book, I found myself thinking about my mom. I even began jotting down "Mom," "Mom," "Mom," in the margins next to passages that reminded me of her. In that particular section, Caroline was giving an example of a how a woman she knew processed conflict in her life, and how that woman emotionally buried the conflicts in her relationships. She described it as an ongoing cycle of unrest. The woman she was writing about really was strangely similar to my mother. In the last line of that section, Caroline stated that someone like this typically develops breast cancer in her later years. My jaw dropped. It had been two years since my mom had a double mastectomy. This was when I started to realize that, as Ms. Myss says, our biography really does become our biology.

The Emotion and Money Connection

I began to read more on the subject of mind and body. I began to understand the connection between our thoughts and emotions and our biology, and I started to see a connection between our emotions and money. One day, I got a call from a client who informed me that he was ill. He had developed bone cancer in his hip. I got a funny feeling that I'd heard this before. I stopped to reflect for a moment. This wasn't the first male client of mine who developed some sort of disease in the hip area. I realized that half of all my male clients between the ages of 55 and 65 had developed some type of problem in their hip area or lower intestines. After looking at this a bit closer, I realized that all these men had been prematurely separated from their life's work. One was let go from a large software company after more than thirty years of service, long before he was emotionally ready to go. I believe that these hard-working, dedicated men became ill in the same physical region because that portion of the body, according to Eastern medicine, is the root chakra. These men got sick because of the emotional toxins that clogged their lower chakra's energy flow as a result of losing their role as the family provider, which was their life's purpose, their ability to work and care for their loved ones.

The Happiness and Health Connection

Later that year, I studied the work of Dr. Deepak Chopra, the bestselling author and co-founder with Dr. Simon of The Chopra Center for Wellbeing. In his book *Power, Freedom and Grace: Living from the Source of Lasting Happiness* (Amber-Allen Publishing: July 31, 2006), Dr. Chopra talks about a cancer patient who came to him for help. Deepak asked him, "Why are you here?" The man said, basically, "I'm here because I want to be cured," to which Deepak responded, "Why do you want to be cured?" The man replied, because he wants to live. Deepak kept digging. "Why do you want to live?" he asked. The patient said that he wanted to live to provide for his family. After quite some time and gentle probing, it became clear that this man wanted to live so that he could provide for his family because *that's what made him happy.* I have found through all of my research into Eastern teachings that happiness is the key to a healthy mind and body. When you're happy inside, your cells regenerate more quickly, and your hormones flow in concert with thriving internal organs. All of the body's systems are positively affected. Sadly though, I don't hear many people say that they are truly happy these days. Do you?

The story about Dr. Chopra and his patient illustrates a primary difference between Western and Eastern beliefs. Western culture wants a cure or a quick fix and, as a result, has us using band-aids for gaping societal wounds. Eastern philosophy seeks to understand what's at the core. In this case, the patient thought he was seeking health, but deep down inside his basic objective was to be happy. By uncovering this truth, Dr. Chopra was able to help the man regain his health by refocusing him on his inner need for happiness—in essence, allowing him to heal himself from the inside out. In my life's journey as a spiritual person, I've discovered that our Western band-aid approach can be incredibly limiting. The ideal solution, I believe, is to take the best of both cultures and merge them to create a phenomenal quality of life.

The Body's Seven Zones of Energy

Eastern philosophy teaches that the human body consists of seven zones of energy. These zones are called chakras (see Figure 3). They are part of the machinery of the body and function on two levels: in the physical realm and in an unseen energy field that flows through the body. My understanding of quantum physics or molecular biology is limited at best, but that a human energy field exists has become much more accepted throughout the scientific community. In fact, recent advances in DNA research have unlocked radically new ontologies in the realm of medicine, chemistry and the origins of disease.

The ancient healers of India upheld the concept that the body consists of seven main and five minor chakras. For the purpose of this book, I'm only going to touch on the seven major chakras, while focusing mainly on the first three—also known as the chakras for processing emotion. If you're interested in learning more about this fascinating aspect of ancient Eastern teaching, please take a look at Appendix 2.

A Toxic Warehouse

Each chakra is a home base for a specific region of the body and its corresponding aspect of life. The seventh chakra, for example, is located at the top of the head. It's the threshold for all things spiritual entering and exiting the body. It's the home of our spiritual energy and in the physical realm corresponds with the brain. Down at the base of your spine is the first chakra. This is the energy center of your foundation, your roots—in essence, your origin. The energy flowing in and out of this chakra zone is tribal in nature. Anything to do with family or group-oriented beliefs is based here. Maintaining a clear energetic flow through this first chakra is crucial to enlightenment because this is where the foundation is laid for your whole being. Modern energetic practitioners will tell you that enlightenment comes from allowing energy to flow freely through the seven chakras, which are also gateways to understanding the mind/body connection. This requires not only tremendous focus and self-awareness, but also calls for an ability to process the toxic emotions we talked about earlier.

Our emotional processing occurs in our first three chakras, while knowledge and intuition are processed through our fifth, sixth and seventh chakras. If you don't recognize the emotions present in your body and work through them, they will build up in a particular chakra region. Imagine barrels of toxins stored in a warehouse. The body is finite like a warehouse; the chakra areas can run out of room. Once the storage space in a chakra area is full, cramming more in can cause an overflow and you could have

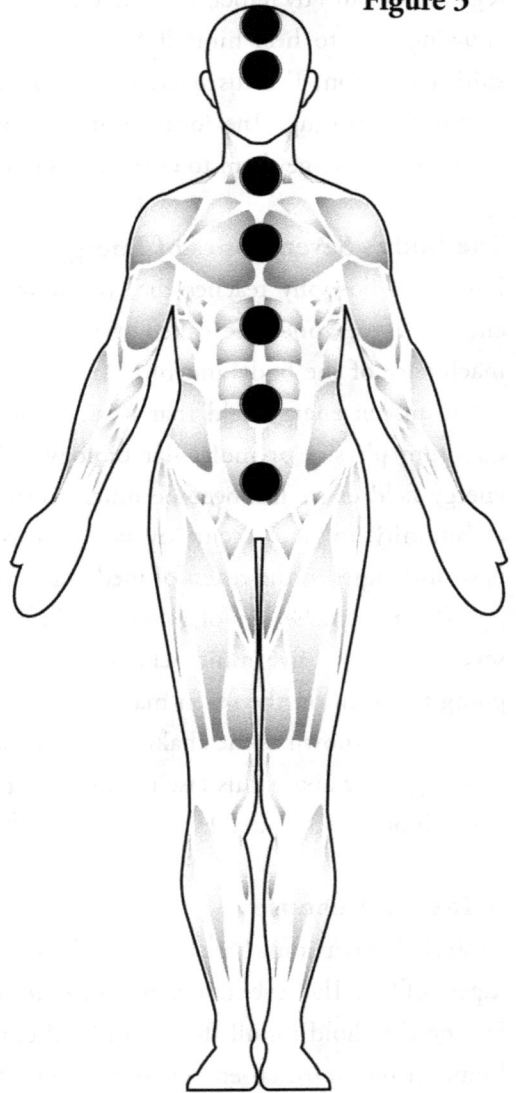

Figure 3

a deadly mess on your hands (or in your stomach, your heart, your reproductive organs or your brain). In the realm of the first or tribal chakra, we must learn to respond to tribal beliefs in a way that does not disrupt the flow of energy around the base of our spine. According to Eastern philosophy, this means releasing deeply imbedded community or family external beliefs and looking beyond the good of the whole to find what's beneficial for you as the unique individual you are.

Getting Out of a Rut

After my dad suffered his two strokes, he became difficult to be around because of his negativity. For months he was not easy to get along with. In his eyes, life was not good. After three months in intensive care and three months in a rehabilitation facility, the rest of us were just happy to have him alive, but that wasn't enough for him. Any effort to lift his spirits fell flat. It seemed that all he could do was complain. Eventually, my mom and I and each of my siblings concluded that we couldn't help him any longer. We were all tapped out. He needed to find the will to live inside himself.

After hearing the same complaints over and over again, it seemed like Dad was keeping an itemized mental list of things that weren't going right, and it was endless! Still, I continued to believe that there was a spark of happiness in him, which once in a while, you could see. He just had to find a way to let it emerge. I remember asking him once how he was, and, as usual, he began reciting all the things that were wrong in his life and what he hated about his situation. I felt so frustrated that I let out a plea. "Dad, isn't there *anything* in your life that's good anymore?" He looked a little surprised, but at that moment a tiny window opened into his soul allowing a sparkle of hope to escape. With a disgruntled look on his face, he declared, "Well, I'm sure glad I'm not in that darn wheelchair anymore!" Ever so slowly, he began seeking out other things that made him happy. Sure, he still has a "crabby list" and some days are better than others. Now when I talk to him, he usually catches himself and tries to identify something that's going well. This is heart-warming. The dad I love and adore is coming back. We all get stuck in various ruts. Some of them can be pretty deep and painful. But one of the wonderful miracles of the human condition is that happiness is our birthright. We have the ability to escape the doldrums of life and return to the bliss we were born with.

Actually, happiness is a funny thing. Just like the interest that compounds in a savings account, happiness grows exponentially. It has a ripple effect. It also feeds on happy behavior. One day in the office, my staff was really stressed out. I pulled out a sheet of smiley-face stickers and walked around putting them on everybody and everything. We all couldn't help but laugh. In one silly moment, the whole mood changed. What's important to recognize is that all you need is one happy moment to carry into the next and the next and so on. Soon you have a whole string of happy moments that keep building on each other. Remember, it only takes one tiny giggle to inspire a big burst of laughter.

You Get What You Give

We've all heard of "karma" in one sense or another. You can have good karma or bad karma. Karma is the memory of some action in your life that creates a desire, which then leads us to action. Your action creates another memory which creates another desire which leads to additional action, and so on. It's a cycle, and you can choose whether it will be a vicious or nurturing cycle. We can also view karma as good or bad. I choose to look at it in a positive manner. How do I create more good karma in my life? Since I was a child, I've heard that you get back what you give in life. I've come to believe this is true, more than I could ever have imagined. It's true that every life has its share of sadness and grief, but it's said that sorrow carves places in your heart that can be filled with joy. If you let yourself hold on to whatever has made you unhappy, you'll create more unhappiness in yourself and in others. If you choose to be happy, regardless of external events occurring in your life, you'll create more happiness for you and for others. Makes sense to me!

Finding happiness begins with recognizing your participation in your own life. Take responsibility for your own happiness. Sometimes being happy can simply be choosing to take some time out for yourself—no TV, no iPod, no kids, no spouse, no radio—just you and your thoughts. Go for a walk or sit quietly at home, in your office, or in your car and just ask yourself, "What would really, truly make me happy?" Even if the answer is, "I'm not sure, I just know that I don't like my life the way that it is now," that's okay. You're on your way to a better place.

6 EXERCISE

Happiness Exercise

Pretty much all of us have one thing that we believe will make us happy. My dad thinks he'd be happy if he could go back to work. "It's awful sitting around the house because then you just get old and die," he says. So, it's time to think about what happiness is to you. Sit quietly and ask yourself, "Am I happy?" If not, why not? Do you want to be happy? Do you believe you can have or deserve happiness? What if you were the man who sought healing from Dr. Chopra and he asked you why you want to live? What would you say? What do you live for? That's quite a daunting question, isn't it? Close your eyes and think back to a time in your life when you were truly happy. You may have to dig, but we've all had some sparkle that occurred at some time. What is it? Relive the joy you felt. Feel it tickling your heart. What was happening in your life at the time? What was the source of your joy? Consider what you can do in your life now to re-create that time or moment of bliss. Write your thoughts down just as they come.

The Skinny on My Weight

After finishing my MBA program in 2005, I began to notice that I had developed somewhat of a weight problem or "challenge" as I prefer to call it. Actually, I got fat. I was the fattest I'd ever been. Why? Well, you could say it was because I was working all the time, eating crappy food and not exercising properly. Throughout my life I've been on and off innumerable diets. I considered myself a Weight Watchers junkie. What I came to learn through my Eastern studies was that my eating habits and my work-centric lifestyle were just symptoms of a deeper need. So any diet I tried was just focusing on the symptom: my unhealthy eating habits. After many months of soul searching, and seven times on Weight Watchers, I realized that there was something going on deep within me that I had not addressed. I had a desire to widen my scope in the business.

I felt driven to create change in the financial services industry and help people heal their relationship with money on a massive scale. Something inside always gnawed at me because I was doing things in a small arena; I also knew in my heart that God didn't give me this personality to do something small.

Until I decided to get out of my own way and give myself permission to explore what this desire was really all about, I was going to continue burying my feelings in unprocessed emotions within my physical body, creating an overweight physique. It was a very scary place to be. I knew I needed some support, so I hired a coach. Taking one step at a time, I began to discover what this desire was all about. Once I found that my happiness was tied to certain ambitions and goals, I shifted my focus inward to accomplish them, and the pounds began to fly off! I didn't even have to diet. It seemed counterintuitive to me, but I'm here to tell you, that I'm living proof. In just six months, I shed 45 pounds and I'm still losing weight today. This may sound strange, but it's as if, by not speaking my truth, my body was warehousing the years and years of financial knowledge and experience I had ingested, storing it in the form of physical fat. Once I was able to eliminate the emotional build-up and openly express my desire to create a change in the industry, the physical weight came off too. Absolutely mind-blowing!

Remember what Dr. David Simon said? Over 90% of the toxins in your body are the result of toxic emotions. I believe that inner healing leads to outward health and I believe bringing peace to your inner emotions is the place where healing begins. I'm not saying that you need to run off and live in an ashram. I'm simply suggesting that *you* bring the concept of inner peace and harmony into *your* home, *your* office, *your* hobbies, clubs and organizations. Better yet, embrace it with your heart. Be rich in whatever it is *you* value and not what our society values. The only way to be permanently successful in your financial life is to start looking inward—to recognize the life you dream about, to live your life's purpose, to love your career (or as Oprah says, "Live your best life") in order to have the life balance that's important to *you*. You'll begin to get into the flow of your own life and be free to develop the financial life you want.

Finding Your Balance

So what exactly do I mean by harmony or balance? You are a unique and complex individual, a biological stew of vibrating molecules, busy hormones and electrically-charged neural synapses, not to mention a spiritual being with your own hopes, dreams, fears and passions. For a variety of reasons, such as your upbringing and biology, along with your psychological makeup, you have chosen to follow a particular life path. Maybe you married young and went to work for a mid-size or large company and you're still there 20 years later, busting your butt to get your kids through college. Maybe you're a single parent, self-employed and nervous about trying to get additional clients. Perhaps your work takes a backseat to the pleasures of life, and you're drawn to the serenity of gardening or the rush of skiing a double black diamond slope. Whether you were raised in an upper-middle-class family or grew up dirt poor and had to eke out a living from practically nothing, the basic truth here is that these different threads of your existence are tightly interwoven and have created the one-of-a-kind tapestry that is you.

Because you're just one person, you can't separate the part of you that loves Edy's Mint Chocolate Chip ice cream from the you that feels threatened on the job by a new boss who is fifty pounds lighter than you and has perfect teeth! They're all pieces of the same whole, and all of these different thoughts and feelings impact each other. This means that you can't be one person in your family life, another in your personal life, and yet another in your work life. That's why when you're frustrated at the office, it shows up at home, in your eating habits or in your relationship with your loved ones. The same is true for how you are with money. The events and dramas of your personal life trickle (or gush) into your financial life. It's that simple. So unless you begin to understand how to get in touch with yourself, your whole self, and unplug from the patterns of behavior that are not in alignment with who you truly are, you'll never achieve genuine happiness. This, in my book, means that you'll also never achieve your full potential financially.

Balance or harmony, therefore, is being in the right relationship with your authentic self. We can achieve the right relationship with our core when we allow the four areas of our lives to function in sync with who we really are. Here are some examples of what I mean.

I. When your *Family Life* is aligned with your true self, you will no longer let your upbringing define you. Nor will you allow your family and their opinions about you determine how you behave.

II. When your *Work Life* is in harmony with your true self, you will no longer let your career, your job title or the size of your office define your purpose or status in life.

III. When your *Personal Life* is in harmony with your core, you'll be able to spend time doing what you truly enjoy. You will also experience a healthier body.

IV. Finally, when your *Financial Life* is guided by your true self and your life's passions, you will no longer surrender your personal power to money. You will know in your heart that happiness isn't purchased; it blooms from within, like a brilliant and beautiful flower.

In Chapters Five and Six, I'm going to take you through a process that will help you align the four areas of your life with your authentic self, your Inner Wealth. For now, though, I want you to start to discover how and why the different parts of your being are not harmonizing with who you really are at your core. The following exercise should help. You'll need a piece of paper and a quiet place to sit. I think you will find it most illuminating.

7 EXERCISE

Harmony Exercise

Sit down, close your eyes, take a deep breath and ask yourself the question, "Who am I?" Write down the first thing that pops into your head. Put it at the top of the page. This should not be how others define you. It's who you feel you are. If you get stuck, write a list of synonyms and adjectives describing yourself, such as teacher, enthusiast, innovator, patient, guardian, graceful, motivator, brave, reverent, trustworthy, etc. Now, write down what you believe to be your purpose in life. Make it personal. No matter how big or small it may seem, write down what feels real to you. You are the only one who matters here. Perhaps you feel your purpose is to raise honest, hardworking children to carry on the family name. Maybe you believe you were put here to make other people laugh. Or maybe your whole reason for living is tied to leading others to physical, emotional or financial well-being.

Now, let's see if your sense of self and life's purpose are in harmony with what happens in the harsh daylight of everyday life.

Make four circles and label them Personal Life, Work Life, Family Life and Financial Life. Next to each circle, I want you to write down your current reality, good and bad, as it applies to each area. For example, in your Work Life circle you might write something like, "I don't enjoy my job." Think about what it is that you like or don't like about your job, and write those specifics down as well. Dig down. Here are some possibilities:

"I'm expected to work overtime but I don't get paid for it."

"I travel too much."

"I love taking business trips."

"My boss loves me."

"My company is unethical."

"My office has an amazing view."

Now I want you to compare the statements you wrote down in your current reality circles to your life's purpose and the words you used to define yourself. For example, maybe you described yourself as outgoing and fun, but in your Personal life circle, you wrote down that you don't get asked out on many dates. Or one of your adjectives was that you're a passionate person, yet in your work circle you wrote that you're bored to tears in your uncreative job.

What did you find? Please don't feel disheartened. Self-enlightenment is often a difficult process. The key here is to see who you are and then begin to unify your reality with the real you.

CHAPTER WRAP-UP

Western culture has us believing that wealth is measured from the outside, that "things" and "stuff" bring happiness.

Many of us today live in a cycle of constant struggle. We are trapped in a perpetual-motion wheel that cycles us through earning more to get more, over and over again.

Financial accountability is not a principle that our society upholds. The savings rate in America recently dipped below what it was during the Great Depression.

Credit cards bring a false sense of financial reality. They make us less conscious of where our money is flowing. Try going for a few months without using a credit card and only paying cash. Your spending level will likely go down significantly.

The cycle of constant struggle to earn cash so you can keep spending takes its toll physically. Our bodies respond negatively to the stress of constant acquisition, from weight gain to heart problems to depression and more. A merging of Western and Eastern medicine philosophies can teach us how our physical health is tied to our life's purpose and sense of happiness.

Many people use acquisition as a source of happiness. Sooner or later the happiness fades and you're left searching for deeper self-fulfillment.

You will remain trapped in this cycle of want until two things occur: One, you discover what truly makes you happy; and two, you learn to live your everyday life in harmony with your authentic self.

"Our past is a story existing only in our minds. Look, analyze, understand, and forgive. Then, as quickly as possible, chuck it."

—Marianne Williamson

3

BREAKING AWAY FROM INHERITED BELIEFS

In the Western world we are taught to honor our fathers and mothers, which is certainly reasonable, but this honor may or may not continue to evolve as we become adults. There's an old saying that childhood is short but its effects last a lifetime. As children, we're told to not question authority, especially that of our parents. The kid asks why he has to do something. "Because I said so!" the harried parent retorts. "Do as you're told." But the time comes when this training may have to be unlearned. I am not a psychologist, physician or pastor, but I am experienced in seeing how our earliest interaction with family and community impacts our financial health. Trust me, I've seen it all and I'm here to tell you that we all have to put away certain hangovers from our childhoods. If you want to achieve your best life financially, you have to let go of those inherited beliefs, fears or behaviors that you picked up from the primary caregivers of your youth that may no longer match your internal wiring. Just as the path to spiritual enlightenment calls for the shedding of certain tribal comforts or beliefs, so does the road to financial health.

My Tribal Issues

Those of you of Irish decent will probably know what I mean when I say "deny" and "repress." I grew up hearing how we Irish folks knew how to work hard in order to survive. This is our heritage. We're the people who'll do whatever it takes to provide for our loved ones. It was also made clear to me that my birthright included turning a blind eye to one's own personal needs; you have to give yourself up for the good of the whole. Sacrifice, sacrifice, sacrifice! This is how I learned to exist in the world throughout my early years. As I mentioned before, I worked my butt off to earn wages that I chose to hand over to my family. That kind of set-up can create a lot of pent-up anger. To deal with it, I made some instinctive compensations; for example, I overate in an attempt to ease my emotional discomfort.

Rebel or Redesign?

Once I went off to college, however, my eyes were opened to a new reality that was different from the arduous life of constant work and silent suffering I had known as a child. I was studying, living and interacting with literally thousands of students who had succeeded in life without having to necessarily toil and struggle to survive. I soon found myself breaking away from my tribal beliefs and questioning my family's attitudes about everything—especially money. Why should I keep sending my hard-earned cash back home? Who says you have to take care of everybody else? What about me and what I want? These thoughts stirred up a great deal of internal conflict. My roommate's father said to me one day, "Julie, you can help your family much more if you help yourself first. If you don't, you'll just keep struggling along with them."

I started thinking of my family back home as a black hole, and I was afraid that I'd get sucked back into it unless I chose a different route. I had yet to learn how to express that internal emotional struggle outwardly. Consequently, those toxic emotions built up inside and began weighing heavily on my lower back. By my senior year, I was spending money on whatever I wanted, forsaking my family for pizzas and colas and sporting events with friends. Throughout the next decade, I was continually suffering from severe lower back pain, to the point that I couldn't walk from my bed to the bathroom. I now know it was no coincidence that the guilt I was harboring about not caring for my family manifested itself in my lower spine, the region of the first chakra. I had compressed my emotions in my lower vertebrae, and cut off the flow of energy there. Mind you, it wasn't my rejection of their communal beliefs that caused the problem. It was that I failed to bring those uncomfortable emotions to the surface. In fact, I created my back pain by living by my inherited beliefs, not by my internal financial beliefs.

Your Financial Upbringing

It will probably come as no surprise to you that parents are *the* biggest influence on our emotions as adults. Your mom and dad, or closest caregivers, were there sending you a money vibe long before you even thought about opening a checking account. You observed their facial expressions and body language, and you heard discussions or arguments about the family finances. What's more, they kept on influencing you long after you left home. That some of these influences are counterproductive to your emotional, physical or spiritual development is not a basis to judge your parents; it's just something to be aware of (and possibly get rid of) in the pursuit of your own happiness.

In one of the classes I teach, we cover the "sandwich generation." These are the baby boomers whose children are still dependent on them for food, clothing or shelter, or all of the above. These same boomer parents have parents of their own who are now getting on in years, and often are also dependent on them for physical, emotional or financial assistance. If you're in this situation, you know all too well that at least one of your folks, if not both, is still advising you about how to handle your affairs *and* theirs. It never seems to end. So there you are, sandwiched between two generations of loved ones who need you.

Finding Your Own Way

Whenever I meet a new client for the first time and begin to ask questions about his or her financial life, I can instantly see what their financial upbringing was like. Children of savers typically become spenders. Parents who are wealthy and buy everything for their kids commonly produce adults who know how to create wealth but aren't so good at keeping it. They're like leaky containers; the money just keeps seeping out. Here's an eye-opening statistic from the U.S. Trust website: Of the people who have a net worth of five million dollars or more (not including their primary residence), 84% of them built their wealth from scratch. That part is great. In those families, by the fourth generation, all those millions are typically gone. That's because no one taught the children of those millionaires how to hold money in abundance. Adults who come from no money at all, and had jobs early on in life, make the best entrepreneurs, because they know how to work hard. I'm living proof of that. Today I work hard and am not afraid to take risks. I'm dedicated to doing whatever it takes to avoid the life of struggle and lack that I knew as a kid, because I'm sure not going there again!

8 EXERCISE

Financial Upbringing Exercise

I'd like you to visualize your childhood for a moment. Picture the house you lived in. Maybe it wasn't even a house but an apartment or condo. What was it like? Modest and cozy or gargantuan and imposing? Or maybe just something in between? Did you have lots of stuff—a TV in every room, the latest techie toys and more clothes than you'd ever need or want? Or was it that you didn't always get what you wanted and were envious of the other kids at school who seemed to have it all? Did you have your own room with your own stuff or did you share a bedroom, bathroom and practically every waking moment with multiple siblings? Was your home beautifully decorated but you never felt at home because you couldn't walk on the carpet or sit on the sofa? Spend a few minutes mentally walking through that home and reliving the conversations that occurred in your home. Try to get in touch with the feelings that accompany you on your virtual tour. Write down whatever comes to mind.

Reflect on your childhood experiences with money. Did you receive an allowance for doing chores, or did it seem like your folks had a magical spigot that spewed out cash whenever they tapped it? Were your folks miserly, pinching every penny, even though there was plenty of cash to go around? Was good behavior in your home rewarded with a trip to the mall to buy a new outfit or sports gear? Did you have a savings account as a kid? How about an investment account? What did your mom and dad or primary caregiver teach you about money? Did you hear a lot of arguing and complaining about money? Did you experience a home filled with gratitude for even the smallest blessing? Just sit quietly and remember. When you're done, take a deep breath and tune in to your current life for a minute. Do you see any recurring patterns between how you were raised and the world you've created? Are there similarities between your spending habits today and how your family dealt with money? Perhaps there are no similarities at all because you vowed, as I did, not to recreate the financial life you knew as a child. And if you have re-created it, how do you want it to change? Above all, remember not to judge yourself. Just notice what feelings come up for you and acknowledge them for what they are—your personal emotions behind money.

Jen's Story

I've known Jen for about ten years now. Her parents did a wonderful job of teaching her how to attract wealth. But when she first came to me for help managing her funds, I realized that nobody had taught her the value of a dollar. She was great at attracting money from an income perspective, so she was income affluent, but she was having difficulty building on that wealth. She was truly in survival mode, and it was an ongoing cycle for Jen. The first trouble spot I found was that when she began her career, she wanted to mimic the wealthy lifestyle that she had experienced living at home with her parents. Unfortunately, she didn't have the income to support that. Consequently, she had accumulated quite a bit of debt—which, unfortunately, Mom and Dad kept paying off for her, so she never learned the lesson of living within her means. When I pointed this out, she said, "But I'm just doing what everybody else does." She kept re-creating debt in her life for two reasons: one, so she could maintain the lifestyle she'd had as a child, and two, so she'd be able to keep up with—you guessed it—the Joneses. She went so far as to pay $210 a month for a haircut, all because she was afraid of not seeming as well-off or better off than her parents or peers. Next to eating and breathing, re-creating the familiar is a primal urge. Every one of us does things in our lives to replicate something we felt or experienced in our childhood. We live in repetitive cycles that are difficult to break.

A Successful Plan

I'm happy to report that today Jen is thriving and practically debt-free. She hasn't had a debt issue for years. After we began meeting, and I took her through the process of putting all aspects of her life in harmony with her heart, she made some important changes in her financial behavior. Together, we created a system for her to follow. After getting a raise, one-third of her raise went toward paying off her debt, one-third went toward building her wealth, and one-third was spent on her lifestyle. Then we created a second system. Now that the debt is gone, she puts one-half of each raise toward her lifestyle and one-half to increasing her wealth. She's done a phenomenal job and, interestingly enough, she married a man who's a good saver, illustrating that she's healing her unhealthy financial emotions, because she attracted a man who supports who she's chosen to be. I'm so happy for Jen. Her new life is helping her grow to the next level in learning how to hold wealth in abundance, because now, not only can she create it herself, she knows how to hold on to it.

Jen didn't change overnight; she re-created her cycle of survival at least five times before she truly had a grasp on her cash flow. The key here is that you have to recognize that once you get a system in place and make major changes in your behavior, setbacks happen. You just have to be willing to hop back on the horse and keep riding.

Unmet Needs and Violated Boundaries

People deal with the stresses of life in different ways. Some shop, some eat, some gamble, some don't eat at all, some drink alcohol, some excessively exercise, some use drugs. Many people today don't have the family or community foundations to assist them in processing life's challenges. There's a level of intimacy missing in our modern world and we're desperately trying to fill the void with something. Our communities are not as close as they once were. We're all too busy. Life is occurring at the speed of light. We're overworked, and that leaves us trying to eat, drink, spend or buy our way to happiness.

I've come to believe that most unhealthy behaviors are the result of emotional conflict or unrest within the individual. There are many differing theories about what triggers those inner stresses. As I explained earlier, I subscribe to the teachings of Deepak Chopra and David Simon, who believe that emotional unrest, or emotional "turbulence" as they call it, results from one of two internal events. The first is having needs that aren't met. The second cause of emotional unrest, they say, is that you may have trouble setting personal boundaries, and in so doing allow your sense of self to be violated.

My little brother Timmy is living proof of the emotional turbulence of unmet needs. The ninth out of twelve children, he didn't always get the level of attention that an active, inquisitive little boy desires. It's not that our folks were bad parents; they just didn't have time to give each child unlimited attention. This was especially hard for Timmy. He learned early on that the only way to get noticed by Mom or Dad was to misbehave. He'd do things like pulling the clean clothes out of our dresser drawers and tossing them all over the room. He would punch or head butt whatever was in his way. He appeared to be such an angry child.

That kind of behavior earned Timmy the attention he craved, even if it was delivered by way of a paddle to his behind. He soon fell into a cycle of bad behavior and punishment. As he grew into adolescence, this cycle created and perpetuated feelings of inadequacy and low self-esteem. If only Timmy had gotten what he really needed—a hug, instead of being screamed at all the time—perhaps he could have avoided some of the struggles he had growing up. There is a happy ending to this story. Today, Timmy is one of the most loving guys you'll ever meet. For some reason, I connected with Tim as an adolescent and was able to provide some TLC for him when he needed it. Eventually Tim went away to college at the University of Iowa. In his junior year he said to me, "You know, Jules, I'm here because of you." I had no idea he felt that way. Today, he's one of my best friends. Life is amazing, isn't it? You just never know how you'll impact another person.

Stay in Touch with Yourself

Modern life doesn't allow us the luxury of time to sort out our feelings or to calm our minds enough to think about our wants and needs. We just go from one routine or event to another with little decompression time, only to explode or implode later when those wants or needs aren't fulfilled. Whenever I sit down with new clients and ask them what it is they truly want out of life, many of them look at me dumbfounded. Running from here to there, we've all ignored or numbed our feelings out of what we chalk up to "necessities." We're not in touch with our own needs. Just as going to the gym to work out or bicycling or jogging is good for our bodies, our minds need that stimulus, exercise and release as well—and the solitude or peace to find it. When was the last time you took yourself for a nice long walk, or created a space at home to be alone with your thoughts?

I'm a firm believer in meditation and prayer as a way to get in touch with one's inner voice and sense of self. The simple act of sitting quietly and listening to your own heartbeat creates a feeling of tranquility; it's a gift you should give yourself daily. Let me give you a personal example. Often when I come home from a long day at work, it's dark outside, particularly during the long winter months in Chicago. I step into my condo and look out the front windows, where I have the most captivating view of Lake Michigan. I love to come home and not flip a single switch—not the lights or the TV or the answering machine. For about five minutes, I just sit in silence and enjoy the beauty of the moon's shimmering reflection on the water. It puts me in a place where I can meditate about my life and get in touch with my soul's desires.

Personal Boundaries

Infants have no boundaries between themselves and, especially, their mothers. The process of separation from parents takes place gradually. As children, we're taught that setting our own personal boundaries is selfish. Many people don't learn that it's okay to say "no" until they're in their forties or fifties. I can't tell you how long it took me to have the gumption to say "I'm not okay with that" to anyone. Still, you know in your heart of hearts if something is acceptable to you; you're either comfortable with it or you're not. Your own intuition is never going to steer you wrong. Give yourself time to listen to your inner voice. Learn to follow your gut without fear of what others might think. After all, they're not you. And remember, you're not them either.

Giving and Taking

As a child I was taught that giving is good, even if it means that you're left with practically nothing. You give and you give and you give, and when you think you've got nothing left, you give some more. Being raised Irish Catholic I was always taught to sacrifice for others, especially family. After all, "Nothing is thicker than blood," as my dad used to say. As I mentioned earlier, while I was in college at the University of Illinois, I used to send money home for my brothers and sisters. After a while, I stopped doing that, but once I got out of college, what do you think I did? I surrounded myself with friends who were takers, not givers. I re-created the familiar pattern from my childhood. My upbringing turned me into the girl who always picked up the tab.

This became painfully real to me two years after graduation. I had this one friend, Jill. We went out together every Friday night. The night almost always began with a nice dinner. Whenever it came time to pay, she would always give me cash for her portion and I would pay the bill with my debit card. I never looked at the bill. I always believed that she had both of our interests at heart. One day, it dawned on me that maybe I *should be* checking to see if we were splitting it down the middle. I soon came to realize that for two years, every single Friday, I had paid all the tax and the tip while Jill just paid for her meal and drinks. I felt like a complete idiot. My trust had been violated. I wondered how someone I considered a good friend could do this to me!

The next Friday night we had a really great time together and then the bill came. I picked it up and handed it to her. It came to $180 and I told her that she needed to pick up the tab for all of the times she left me to pay all the taxes and tips. Jill knew exactly what she had been doing and she paid the bill without any argument. I just hadn't set a boundary so that I would not be taken advantage of. We still laugh about it, and once in a while she even picks up the whole check. It also had never occurred to her that the reason she let other people pay more was due to the fear she had of not having enough money for her life. To be fair, Jill and I were both caught up in our own emotional baggage.

Sometimes it just takes the courage to have open and honest communication about a situation. Certainly, some people who trespass your boundaries may not stay in your life, but that's fine. People come and go in our lives for reasons. The way I see it, everyone comes into our lives to help us on our journey, and to help us become more of who we really are.

Boundary Lessons

The real issue for me here, however, had little to do with Jill's underpayment. I clearly had a problem setting boundaries. I was reluctant to look after myself. I never suggested that we alternate paying the tab. I never even checked the bill to see what I actually owed. I chose to play the victim instead of taking responsibility for my own actions. Like most people, some lessons don't come easy for me. A few years after my boundary-setting revelations with Jill, I found myself at my first job out of college with another boundary issue, but this time I had some help. I worked my way onto the fast track fairly quickly, yet money still burned a hole in my pocket, just as it did when I was twelve, and just as it has with my parents throughout their lives. The faster it came in, the faster it went out. This was no secret to my friends and colleagues at the office. Leeda was a young graduate I mentored. She was a strong personality like me and, to this day, I'm convinced that she came into my life to teach me some lessons about cash flow. Leeda sat me down one day and said, "Julie, I think you need a personal budget." I was shocked. The student was going to teach the mentor something about finance? Right there on the spot, Leeda helped me create a budget for my personal life and said that she was going to hold me accountable to it!

We decided that I would have $160 per week to spend on eating out and entertainment. The first week I took $160 out of the cash machine on Monday morning. It was gone by Wednesday, but I vowed to stick to the plan. I had agreed to that amount, I wasn't forced into it. Once again I reminded myself that if you always do what you've always done, you'll always get the same results, and I really wanted to change. I wanted a new reality. I stayed in that weekend, which was the hardest lesson on money I had learned, particularly in my early twenties. The following Monday, I grabbed my next $160 cash. This week it lasted until Thursday. The third Monday of my new reality I took $160 out of the bank. This time I was very excited to have $20 left to spend on Friday night. The fourth week, I had $40 to go wild with on Saturday night. Finally, five weeks after I sat down with Leeda, I was able to shift my priorities to spend $160 per week on eating out and entertainment. Now some people would say that's a lot of money, but, this was my financial roadmap, no one else's. I realized that I paid everyone else before I paid myself, meaning I was buying lunches, dinners, drinks—you name it, I paid for it. I suppose, looking at it now, I was a great person to go out with because the other person never spent any money. Over time, I had extra money every week and was soon able to plan for other items I wanted to buy.

Saying "No" to Them and "Yes" to You

This exercise also made me realize that I had resumed the financial rescue mission with my family. I was spending $1,000 per month on my siblings, from buying them school supplies and clothes to taking them out for dinner. Leeda and I agreed that I would only spend $35 per week on my family. I couldn't cut them off completely because I'm a giver at heart and enjoy being one. Leeda's stand was this. "Julie," she said, "you can help your family more by helping yourself first." This was the second time in my life I was advised to help myself first, *then* go back and help the family. Now I know why. You need to stabilize *yourself* before you can assist others; otherwise you're left vulnerable and at risk too, and that doesn't do anyone any good. It's like the friendly flight attendant instructing you to put your own oxygen mask on first before helping your child or another passenger with theirs. Soon I was able to say to my family, "Okay, I have $35 to spend this week on you guys and when it's spent, there's no more." I had to announce this cutback to every member of my family because, emotionally, I felt uncomfortable and guilty about it. I hoped that saying it out loud would help me stick to my own resolution.

Well, the story doesn't end there. The lesson truly hit home for me when my sister-in-law called a few weeks into my new budget to ask if I was doing anything that Friday. I was excited that someone from the family actually called me to see if I wanted to get together. Since I'd moved downtown, my siblings were rather reluctant to visit me. I now lived in the big city, which was very different from where we grew up. The city was a place they didn't visit on a regular basis. My sister-in-law said, "You haven't seen the kids in a while and we thought we'd come down." I was tickled pink! Then the bomb dropped. She said, "Oh, also, your brother and I are out of money, and we thought that if you haven't spent your $35 this week, you could buy us pizza while we're there." It took all the strength and courage I could muster to speak. I told her that I was sorry but I had already spent my family money that week. They never came over. I was crushed. This was one of the hardest lessons I've ever learned. I was giving away far too much money to other people, and they'd come to expect it from me. What was even more difficult for me was accepting that I was 50% of the problem. I had to learn to set boundaries for myself if I was ever going to have wealth.

Financial Personality Types

Does this sound familiar? You see a kid having a meltdown in the grocery store. His mom is desperately trying to calm him by cajoling or sweet-talking or even by walking away. Finally, she gives in and buys him something just to get him to stop crying. I'm no psychologist, but I believe that buying your way out of a tantrum buys you into a heap of trouble as a parent. You're planting a seed of thought that says money fixes everything. That little seedling can grow into a mighty big behavioral problem. There's a difference between a celebration, such as the whole family going out for ice cream after a winning baseball game, and "paying" a child to stop misbehaving. Whether the reward system is food-based, money-based or otherwise, the behavioral patterns that result from that conditioning will be carried into adulthood.

Every one of us has ways of acting out because of unmet needs or violated boundaries. In my experience as a wealth advisor, I've recognized some pretty amazing demonstrations of rebellion, guilt and fear in people's financial lives. Again, this is nothing to be ashamed of, but it's helpful to recognize what your triggers are so that when they arise, you can choose a different response.

I've come to the conclusion that there are some common financial personalities that are a direct result of different financial upbringings. Here they are, in no particular order.

1. Hoarders—Are you someone who stuffs the sugar packets in your pocket or purse whenever you're at a restaurant? When someone else throws something away, do you take it? Are you territorial when it comes to sharing something of yours with others? What are you protecting? Why are you afraid of loss? I've found that people who gravitate to this type of amassing behavior were typically givers when they were younger. Unfortunately, they wound up surrounding themselves with takers who helped themselves to every personal object they could get their hands on. They also allowed others to take from them financially and emotionally. Over time, resentment and a loss of self began to overshadow their giving spirit. So the hoarder learns to stockpile stuff (and often emotions) out of fear that her things, if not her entire sense of self, will be snatched up by others once again. I've also noticed that hoarders can be those who actually came from very little when they were younger, and when they start to get more financial flow in their lives, they hold onto it with a tight grip for fear that if they don't, they'll go back to where they came from.

2. Spenders—Does money burn a hole in your pocket? As fast as money comes in, is it already spent? Have you amassed a lot of credit card debt and don't really know what you spent your money on? If you have a closet full of outfits with the tags still on them or if your home is filled with gadgets you never use, it's a good bet you're a spender. Emotionally speaking, excessive spending is often linked to inner pain or discomfort. The spender spends money to alleviate an inner need, such as love or acceptance. Of course, buying provides only temporary relief and the spending cycle continues. If you think you're a spender, consider cutting up your credit cards and canceling that line of credit until you can teach yourself how to hold onto cash without spending it. How do you do this? Well, here's a fun little trick I recommend to my spend-happy clients. When you get your next paycheck, go to the bank and get a $100 bill, and put that Benjamin Franklin in your wallet. *Do not spend that $100 under any circumstances.* Watch what emotions come over you. This can be a painful exercise for spenders. It's almost as if old Ben himself is constantly whispering in your ear, "Spend me, spend me, spend me!" If you succumb, which usually happens, try again next pay period. Resist the temptation to spend it as best you can. Keep getting back up on that horse until the emotional urge to spend that money is gone. This will create stress, but it will also force you to deal in a different way with whatever emotions are coming up for you. Believe it or not, eventually you'll become comfortable letting that $100 bill stay in your wallet.

3. Saboteurs—These people are extremists, constantly fluctuating between abundance and scarcity, hoarding and spending. Saboteurs are masters at knocking themselves out of the success realm, spiraling down into a place of lack. This behavior is seldom conscious, and there are many reasons why people sabotage themselves. I've noticed that it often seems to be because way down deep in their subconscious minds, saboteurs really don't believe that they can have financial abundance or that they deserve it. They may know it logically but, emotionally, their actions re-create the familiar—a state of guilt for feeling undeserving. If you're a financial saboteur, you should know that you're greatly influenced by the company you keep. You may be a real go-getter, but you surround yourself with people who are not. This creates an ideal environment for slacking off, a place where it's easy to fit in when you fail. In their heads, saboteurs know they want to live a life of abundance and happiness, but subconsciously, they believe they don't deserve it.<

4. Givers—These are the wonderfully warm, generous souls who keep the world of charity alive. Interestingly enough, givers typically have a hard time receiving. When you don't receive with grace, it limits the positive flow of money in your life. There is always more money going out than coming in. If you're a giver, you're likely to be attracted to spenders or hoarders. If this is your reality, you should understand, in no uncertain terms, that you will forever be trying to fill up someone else's bucket. But alas, you will never be able to fill it, because spenders and hoarders are leaky containers. The only person who can plug a leaky container is the leaky container itself. The giver will continue to give and the spender or hoarder will continue to take. In some respects, you're a perfect match, one feeding off the other. Financially, this cycle must be broken in order for the giver to fully thrive in an abundant life. To heal, givers must learn to set boundaries to keep their giving in a balanced relationship, one that is mutually flowing back and forth between giving and gracefully receiving.

5. Controllers—These folks tend to be frugal in nature. They think about their money situation 24/7 and it's integrated into every aspect of their lives. You won't be likely to find a money controller consulting with a wealth manager. They want to know every detail every step of the way, and they want to be in charge of every decision. Most controllers manage their financial affairs themselves, often with much success, building a great deal of wealth over time. Unfortunately, controllers pay a price for their financial gains, because they're not typically mindful of their personal relationships. They tend to get in their own way. They are micromanagers, all too happy to tell others what to do or driving to numerous stores trying to intimidate the salespeople to get a better deal. This behavior often gets them what they want in the short term, but the controller's narrow focus distracts him from the big picture This can prove hazardous in every realm of life, both professionally and personally.

6. Planners—Do you find comfort in plotting out how to get from points A to B? Are you always two steps ahead of everyone else in picking a restaurant or vacation destination? Welcome to the well-thought-out world of the planner. Are you always thinking and living in the future, as opposed to living in the present moment? Are you always happy to be the ringleader, to organize parties, meetings, trips and, of course, what to do with your money? Planners are not very spontaneous with their money. They much prefer making careful, steady financial choices and decisions. Their challenge arises when life, as it always does, tosses a curveball. This can really throw the planner off balance. They live so much for the future that they are not living for today. But as we all know, we really only have the present moment. It's a shame to miss it by obsessing about tomorrow. Trust me, I know. I'm a bona fide planner. Yep, that's me. Luckily, I have people in my life that are the most in-the-moment people I've ever known—my ideal life and people that help bring more balance and harmony into my life.

7. Carefree Butterflies—"Oh, it will just find a way to be there." "Somehow it will all work out." These are the catchphrases of the carefree, especially when it comes to money. Carefree folks are uplifting to be around because they don't let the worries of the world bring them down. They're typically healthy, happy individuals in every aspect of life. They live in the present moment. However, without a little guidance and a daily reality pill, Mr. and Ms. Carefree have the potential to become completely disconnected from their money. I find that many moms who choose to stay at home to raise the kids can fall into this category. Oftentimes, they run the house while their husbands handle the money. This is a dangerous situation because, God forbid, if something happens to their spouse, they're lost. They have no realistic relationship with money and are forced to pick up the pieces if and when things fall apart.

8. Attractors—Is money your lifelong friend? Has it always been at your side or in your wallet from as far back as you can remember? Do you profit from every venture you set your mind to? Does everything you touch turn to gold? You're one of the lucky ones, my friend. You're an attractor. You inherently know how to open up the channels in your life. Money comes to you with little effort on your part. Just thinking about success brings bundles of cash and oodles of opportunities to your doorstep. The amazing thing is that the more attractors share their wealth with others, the more wealth comes back to them. They have completely opened the flow in their life—the flow of giving and receiving. What a beautifully healthy cycle!

Find Your Blind Spots

Which one of these personality types do you believe describes you? It may be one or a combination of two or more. Whenever I ask people which types they identify with, I get a lot of sighs and groans. Sometimes it's really hard to admit our financial behavior. Many of us carry a lot of shame or guilt when it comes to who we are financially. Kick that judge off your shoulder so you can see your financial self objectively. My hope is that reading these descriptions will spark an epiphany within your soul, perhaps illuminating a blind spot that you have about your relationship with money. By shining a light on your behavior with money and questioning why you have these tendencies, you're building yourself up for a successful transition into a thriving mode that will allow you to attract wealth.

9 EXERCISE

Financial Blind Spot Exercise

I encourage you to take a few minutes and consider some of these behaviors in light of your current financial health. Reflect back on the last month or pay period. What was going on inside you emotionally? Did those feelings, happy, sad or otherwise, get transferred onto your Visa card? Does your financial personality change depending on who you're with? Search your mind for parallels between your current financial patterns and your upbringing. Consider what relationships or tribal rules and beliefs still have a powerful influence over your financial independence. What would happen if you were to break away from certain financial habits? How do you think you would feel if you changed? How do you think your family and friends would react if you changed? Sit quietly, breathing in and out. Don't judge anyone, especially yourself. Just think and listen to what your heart is saying.

Rebuilding Your Foundation

A dear friend of mine, the gifted psychotherapist Mary Ann Daly, has spent over twenty-five years working in the fields of trauma and addiction recovery. In her upcoming book, *You Are the Change You've Been Waiting For,* she talks about the importance of helping people with histories of childhood trauma to create a new emotional infrastructure. In a course Mary Ann teaches, she conceptualizes three stages of the recovery process that categorize how we respond emotionally to personal tragedy, grief, loss, abuse and trauma.

The first stage she identifies is that of the **Victim.** She explains that people in this part of the recovery process tend to feel stuck, helpless, hopeless, depressed, overwhelmed, afraid and angry. It's a stage that is similar to that of a child because, like children, they experience their situation as one in which they have no control, or no sense of control.

When someone is in a victim stage, they tend to:

- think and speak negatively;

- see things in black and white only;

- be incapable of seeing options to get out of difficult situations;

- display either very low (depressed) or very frantic (anxiety) energy levels;

- often be chronically sick, and/or very disconnected from their bodies; and

- become quite skilled at putting up defenses (denial, justification, aggression, repression, acting out, blaming, fantasizing) as a way of protecting themselves.

Those in the victim state tend to trust people who aren't deserving of their trust. They're unable to trust themselves, and they have little or no sense of purpose in life.

The second stage is the **Survivor.** This is the stage when people in recovery feel more hopeful and motivated to change. They see options and the possibility of things changing for the better. In this stage, recovery patients display adolescent-like thinking and behavior. They show an inability to consistently make mature and healthy choices that reflect an adult's understanding of the laws of consequence. These people live in a place of potential while struggling to accept full responsibility for their actions. Their defense mechanisms include:

- competitive behavior,

- an inability to respect boundaries,

- taking extreme positions, and

- a willingness to live with very negative consequences and, as a result, lapse back into feeling victimized.

Survivors are able to see a relationship between their emotions and their bodies and begin taking better care of themselves physically. They also begin thinking about having a better sense of purpose in their lives, but they aren't clear about what that is for them at the moment. Unlike the victim, they become less anxious and depressed about facing the unknown, which enables them to begin to trust themselves.

The third stage is the **Thriver.** In this stage one is able to function as an adult. People operating at this level are consistently able to express their feelings in appropriate, healthy ways. The defense mechanisms that thrivers demonstrate include:

- clear and solid boundaries and

- the ability to recognize and honor their own limitations and those of others.

Thrivers have good self-discipline. They take regular care of their bodies, viewing them as connected to their mental and emotional well-being. Additionally, they're consistently honest, willing to accept responsibility for the consequences of their mistakes.

Thrivers experience life on life's terms. They welcome change as an opportunity to grow and are capable of finding tools and resources to transform difficulties or pain into gain. They've learned to trust themselves, which gives them the ability to recognize who or what they can and cannot trust. They display gratitude and appreciation regularly, they appreciate and celebrate the differences in others, and they experience life from a place of cooperation rather than competition. Thrivers also possess the faith that somehow they will be taken care of. They are truly individuals who see the glass as half full. Thrivers have a clear sense of purpose and feel a strong connection to their spirit and the universe. This enables them to demonstrate wisdom. They are free from the need to control outcomes, and their energy flows in an easy, free and comfortable manner.

Your Emotional Infrastructure

By tapping into her spiritual gifts of insight and compassion, Mary Ann helps her clients rebuild their psychological and emotional foundations so that they're able to process their emotions more effectively, and eventually progress from feelings of victimization to a sense of personal accountability and self-acceptance. In short, the focus of her work is to help her clients thrive.

One day, while we were having lunch together, she shared with me that sometimes she feels like a psychological plumber. What she meant was that she often has to help people install a new emotional infrastructure or rehab their old ones much like a plumber installs, reroutes or replaces rotted pipes in a home for maximum water flow. She said that people from dysfunctional families often don't have the emotional infrastructure to handle their feelings in healthy, appropriate ways. They tend to either cut off their feelings or become emotionally overwhelmed. A new or improved infrastructure allows us to experience normal feelings of anger, disappointment, regret, sadness, etc. while at the same time feeling emotionally sound.

As we were talking, a light bulb suddenly clicked on in my head. In order to progress from financial victim to survival mode to a sense of thriving, you need a new infrastructure, one that can help you handle your money emotions safely and effectively. You need a master plan based on your personal flow of emotions and your flow of money.

Is Your Foundation Safe?

Since my dad was an electrician, I see it like this: If you want a fully functioning, modern home with power in every room, you need a sound electrical system designed to produce maximum power. But, what if the original structure's electrical system is lacking? Say your home has a faulty fuse box or not enough wire running safely to the right places—how well would that house serve your needs? Or worse, how *safe* is that house? You'd call a skilled professional to help you rewire and show you how to safely use all the power flowing through your walls, right? Do you see the analogy here? Your financial personality is that house, and I'm here to assist with laying a new foundation, one that will give you maximum financial power and flow.

By now I hope you're beginning to see that making money and building wealth isn't something you achieve from following a formula. We make financial decisions on a deeper, more personal level, just as we do to make almost every decision in our lives. In order to achieve wealth in life, you're going to have to make a few adjustments to your own emotional infrastructure. This is radically different thinking from what's currently espoused by some of today's most high-profile money experts. I want you to understand that when you subscribe to some TV guru's prefab, one-size-fits-all financial program for success, you're not in control of your financial destiny. It does not do you a dime of good to emulate the investment strategies of world-famous tycoons and multimillionaire executives. When you do, you're merely surrendering your personal power to them. Certainly you can learn from others, but you have to build your wealth from the inside out, not outside in.

The Struggle for Power

I have a friend who believes that a constant struggle over power and control takes place within every relationship. At any given moment, one of you is in control on some level. Why wouldn't this be true of your relationship with money? At what point in your life did you decide to hand over your own personal power to the almighty dollar, yen, euro, peso or pound? Today, I'm no longer willing to hand over my personal power to anything or anyone, especially when it comes to money. I base my entire business on the concept of the emotion behind money, and the simple fact that you can't help people build a life of wealth and abundance simply by selling them a specific line of products. Oh, sure, there are some people out there who actually have been able to build a small fortune by following some cookie-cutter approach to financial planning. I'd be willing to bet, however, that those people aren't as happy with their lives as they could be. I've become a successful wealth advisor by helping my clients get in touch with their own money emotions, and by exploring who they are as individuals. My aim with my clients is to help them define and focus on their innermost hopes, dreams and desires, and then build a strategy to make these all come true. Anything less is a life based on mere survival, and I believe that anyone with a brain, a heart and a bank account deserves much more than that.

10 | EXERCISE

Surviving to Thriving Exercise

Get a piece of paper and draw a line down the middle, top to bottom. Label the left column "Current Financial Behaviors" and the right column "New Behaviors." Now I'd like you to refer back to the list of Financial Personalities. Read through them again, and when you see a characteristic that rings true for you, write it down. Then list a few examples of situations in which you exhibited that characteristic. For example, I recognize myself as a Giver. The sentence that says, "Givers have a hard time receiving" really strikes a chord with me. I can think of countless times in my life when I felt uncomfortable receiving from others, from birthday gifts to professional accolades. Write down as many scenarios as you can think of. Be specific. Incorporate names and locations if you need to.

When you've made your way through the list of personality types, I'd like you to turn your attention to the right-hand column. Now write down a different response that you could have exhibited with each corresponding situation on the left. For example, I can think of a couple of ways I could have responded differently when I received my first sales award. Instead of downplaying my colleagues' congratulatory remarks, I could have smiled and thanked them graciously. Or I could have strutted around the office like a prize rooster. Or I could have told my boss that I'm uncomfortable with public recognition and I'd rather that he not make a big to-do about it. The point to all of this is that you have choices. Even if you're the biggest Spender or Planner or Controller you know, you have choices in your day-to-day financial behavior. So go ahead, see if there are some habits that you would like change.

CHAPTER WRAP-UP

Your emotions, including your money emotions, are largely a part of your upbringing. Oftentimes, how we choose to respond to our childhood beliefs will eventually come out later in life in the form of poor physical health and/ or unhealthy financial behavior.

Feelings of emotional unrest are typically the result of either unmet needs or a lack of personal boundaries.

Everyone has a financial personality based on their upbringing and their ability to deal with inner conflict.

Everyone has an emotional infrastructure. Some of us need repair work done on that infrastructure so that we're able to process the feelings that may arise from needs that haven't been met, or from boundaries that we feel have been violated.

By focusing on changing our financial behavior, even in the smallest of ways, we begin to progress from a life of victimhood or survival mode to a life of thriving and abundance.

SECTION TWO
Choose to Change

"Find the courage to break those agreements that are fear-based and claim your personal power."

—Don Miguel Ruiz

OWN YOUR PERSONAL POWER

Remember the new Huffy bicycle I earned selling candy for the Midlothian softball team? From that day on, wheels meant freedom to me. When I was just eleven, I started saving for my first car. I figured with a car I'd be as free as a bird. Since the family was always short of funds, the unwritten rule was if you had the cash, you coughed it up for the family. There were many times when my mom and dad asked if I could help out with the household expenses, and I would always say "Yes." I gave up my goals and dreams to give to the family. I was a good little Catholic girl who did her duty. Over time, I started to become resentful because of it. Ask any one of my siblings and they'll tell you they called me "Julie the bitch." While it took a long time to acknowledge the advice I would later get (You'll never really be any good to anyone else financially or emotionally if you don't take care of your own needs first), I somehow intuited it, albeit guiltily. I started to secretly stash away a bit of cash for me. I still gave some to the family, but I allowed myself to see to my own needs too. In essence, even though I felt guilty about it, I was finding a balance between my perceived moral duty and my own true desires in life.

My Dream Car

One day, when I was fifteen, I got into a huge fight with my mom. I don't remember what started it, but I do know I was so angry that I stormed out of the house in an adolescent huff. I went for a long walk, past the modest

Chicago suburban homes, eventually reaching a long string of car dealerships. It was there that I made the first of many decisions that would change my life. There it was in all of its glory—a gray Plymouth Colt parked in a nearby used car lot. I vividly remember walking around and around this car, wondering, hoping and dreaming about myself behind the wheel. Finally, I looked up at it and said aloud, "That's the car I'm going to buy!" I was fifteen years old and had only $2,000 saved, but I resolved right then and there that by the time I was sixteen I'd have wheels. Finally I'd have something that was mine and only mine. That Colt was to be my freedom. Then I looked at the sticker on the window. My heart sank. The price was $8,000, far more than I had in the bank. I wondered how I was ever going to find that freedom I yearned for from the very depths of my being.

I'm not sure what compelled me, but I told my godmother, who's also my aunt, about my dream car, my freedom. I'm not sure if it was my passion or desperation that touched her, but a few days later she called me up and asked me out to dinner with her and my Uncle Matt. They wanted to talk to me about something. Growing up in an Irish Catholic household, I knew that when you were summoned to a "talk," it usually wasn't a good thing. I wondered what I'd done and dreaded our upcoming dinner. What could it be but a one-way ticket to a guilt trip? As it turns out, my fears were completely unfounded. Aunt Jeanne and Uncle Matt told me that they'd decided to loan me the remaining money I needed to buy the car. They put me on a payment plan, and three weeks before my sixteenth birthday, the Plymouth Colt was mine!

From Intention to Reality

This story marks a significant turning point in my life, one that had little to do with the car itself. I learned two valuable lessons that year. First, I learned the value of negotiation. My aunt and uncle actually came with me to the dealership and haggled the price of the car down to one I could afford to make payments on. We'd already decided that $7,000 was the magic number and not a penny more. The dealer agreed and I bought the car. The second lesson I took from this experience was more profound. In reality, that gray Plymouth Colt wasn't what I needed to escape my life of want. My intention, my burning desire to get the heck out of poverty was the key to a new life. I discovered I had a new power, the power of choice. I could choose my life's path. It really was that simple.

Today, I fully believe that life is about choices and that the life you live is *your* choice. Consequently, right now, today, you can consciously choose what your future is going to be. Show me what a person is doing today, and I'll tell you what their future will be. You have a voice and a choice in the health of your financial future. Remember the survival cycle I mentioned earlier? Now that you've recognized the behavior patterns that your relationship with money has created, it's time for you to choose to change. Choose the reality that you, *and only you*, prefer!

The Power of Choosing to Change

I know what you're thinking. In your mind you're saying, "Julie, that's all good and fine, but choosing to create wealth isn't going to pay off the $14,000 balance on my Visa bill or send my children to college. It won't allow me to work fewer hours at my job, or actually be able to spend more time with my grandchildren." Oh yes it will, my friend, because once you choose to change and give that choice dominion over all of your intentions, your financial life will never be the same. Your intentions are very powerful tools in building wealth. Without them, you're just a sitting duck for good or bad luck, a victim of whichever way the wind blows. By setting intentions, and applying practical action to those intentions, you have the power to shift your reality and begin to see positive change right before your eyes. Your energy flows where your energy goes!

Here's a perfect example of this. When I began the quest to reach my benchmark weight, I made friends with the treadmill at the gym. Now, as you probably know, when you step on the machine and push the start button, it asks you a series of questions about your desired workout intensity, target heart rate, etc. It also asks for you to put in your weight. I always entered my ideal, not my actual, weight. Even though the scale told me I had many pounds to lose before I actually weighed that, I still put the number in. Day in and day out, on every visit to the gym, I gave that machine the same data, which over time brought me directly to that weight. In essence, I was changing my reality to be what I *intended* it to be.

Intention as a Power Tool

Your intentions are without doubt the most powerful and crucial aspect of wealth building. An intention is a trigger for change. It's the first pitch in the big game. Setting an intention is a spiritual process. It opens the door to a world where unseen forces busy themselves 24/7 to manifest miracles on your behalf. Intentions set the wheels in motion for a new reality. We've all heard stories about professional athletes who practice their golf swings, free throws or triple axel spins in their heads every day before they ever step foot on the fairway, basketball court or skating rink. In his first book, the semiautobiographical novel *Way of the Peaceful Warrior* (Houghton Mifflin; 1st edition: 1980) Dan Millman, a former world-champion gymnast and human potential coach, wrote of living in the moment in alignment with the heart, free of striving and performance pressure. His story of focus and intent is riveting, and makes clear that without intent, there is no forward motion in our lives. Our goals give birth to motivations that in turn drive us to the finish line. This is especially true with money. Right now, at this very moment, you have the power to change your current reality, simply by turning your desires and dreams into intentions. Over the next few chapters I'm going to show you how.

11 EXERCISE

Choose to Change Exercise

This is a good time for you to consider choices that you'd like to make for your life today. Your future is your choice; you're the designer. What's it going to be? What positive financial choices would you like to make? What unhealthy financial choices would you like to change or completely let go of? Be loving and considerate. Don't use the word "hate" toward yourself or your behavior. My grandfather always said that hate is such a harsh word, and I agree. You may strongly dislike something, but hate is very harsh. So, what do you dislike about your current reality? Think of these dislikes as familiar items that you've outgrown, such as a childhood toy, a piece of furniture or an article of clothing. Close your eyes for a minute and let your mind explore the possibilities. Then write each behavior as the completion of this statement: I choose to _____.

Here are some suggestions:
- *"I choose to love myself enough to lose the excess weight on my body."*
- *"I choose to live within my means."*
- *"I choose to face my current financial reality."*

Or you can simply state your intent:
- *"I choose to save $100 a month for six months."*
- *"I choose to have a positive relationship with money."*
- *"I choose to have wealth in abundance."*

The possibilities are endless because they're your possibilities. After you've made a list, look it over. Pick as many choice statements as you like and write them down on sticky notes. These are your reminders of how you choose to live, financially or otherwise. Post them in places where you'll see them every day. Have fun with it. Heck, plaster your home and office with colorful notes if you like. Say them to yourself throughout the day. It won't be long before those conscious choices are transformed into new behaviors and a new reality.

The Magic of Perspective

There's a quaint little harbor town in Maine called Ogunquit where tourists flock to enjoy the natural beauty of the New England coastline. In addition to its lovely rocky beaches and beautiful sunsets, Ogunquit is a thriving artists' community with unique galleries and gift shops. One afternoon, I found myself wandering through the town's main streets. As I stepped out of a souvenir shop, something caught my eye. On the street corner ahead was a lovely black, silver, and white metal bin with the word "Peace" printed on the side in a friendly typeface. I didn't think too much about it until I saw a second one down the street and later another and yet another. They were all painted the same color, but each bore a different word of inspiration, such as harmony, grace, happiness, joy and peace. These cheerful landmarks were dotted throughout the community, and I soon came to discover that they were the town's public trashcans. I was fascinated by the contrast between each lovely sentiment and the crassness of its canvas—the side of a garbage receptacle.

The point I'm making is that how others see you has everything to do with how you see and portray yourself. We all choose to put our lives in a certain perspective, to play different roles—victim, martyr, hero, child, rich man, poor woman, the list goes on and on. And those roles are who we become.

Two Sides to Everything

I love an old illustration from the Victorian era I remember from my high school days (see Figure 4). At some point in your life you've probably come across it too. It's one of those pictures that play tricks with your mind. Depending on how you look at it, you either see the profile of a young woman or an old hag. I find it amazing that the same image can literally depict two different realities. Your life is that drawing. The image that you're currently focused on is your current reality. If you choose to see a different perspective, your reality would change. This means that a shift in your perception about money yields a different outcome.

Another way to look at this is to consider an argument you've recently had with someone. You remember your side but can you imagine the other's perspective? Most likely, neither side is right or wrong, just different. It would be amazing if more people would first seek to understand and then to be understood, as Steven Covey talks about in his book, *The Seven Habits of Highly Effective People* (Free Press, 2004). We'd have a lot less friction in the world if we actually believed that there's more than one point of view to most matters in life. Because there is!

Figure 4

Keeping Positive

A few years ago, I made a conscious choice to keep a positive perspective on things. I consider it a waste of energy to be anything but peaceful and happy. Every day, especially in the face of hard times, we each have the option to choose to see a hidden blessing or an opportunity to learn a life lesson. One of my vendors complimented me on my cheerful personality, but told me that at first he didn't believe it was natural. "When I first met you," he said, "I thought you wasted so much energy trying to seem happy. No one is naturally that happy. It must be exhausting to keep up the façade." But being happy was not my nature when I started out in the business. It was something I had to teach myself. It was a *choice* I made and still make every day. Don't get me wrong. There are still some days when life hands me a curve ball, and the last thing I want to do is smile. It's just that I no longer let those moments define me for the entire day. I don't think a couple of rain clouds should cast total darkness over an otherwise sunny day. Last time I checked there were twenty-four hours in a day, and I'm not going to let just 8% of it create my reality. Again, it's your choice. Your perception is your reality.

The Language of Your New Reality

Your thoughts aren't the only things that define your reality. The words you choose to express those thoughts shape your existence as well. Your vocabulary can rob you of abundance or shower you with wealth. Do you limit yourself when you talk about your finances? Ever hear yourself say things like, "Oh I could never afford that," or "That's way too expensive for me?" Why do you deny yourself an abundant life? My thought is if talk show hosts and movie stars can make $5 million or more a year, why can't I? Why can't you? You can! Keeping in mind that these talk show hosts and movie stars don't make their millions by waiting for money to fall from trees, you too can be a millionaire. You just need to get out of your own way. Imagine what your life would be like if you never felt anything was untouchable or out of reach. What if the power of your intentions, thoughts and words could actually become your reality? What if when you choose to live a certain life, think of yourself living that life and talk as if it already existed, it becomes real? You are what you think and you are what you say. If you think you're poor, and let your words follow suit, then your actions will eventually produce your reality of being poor. It's called the Law of Attraction, and it's powerful!

Positive thoughts expressed with positive words create—you guessed it—a positive reality. It's amazing how a shift in your internal thoughts and external words can move you away from an unhealthy financial life toward a whole new financial existence. Don't worry yourself with how all of this is going to work right now. Just start to make yourself aware of the limiting thoughts that poison your mind and the negative vocabulary that accompanies those thoughts.

12 EXERCISE

Take Your Passion, and Make It Happen

Get a piece of paper and write down your answer to this question: What would you like to do but feel you'll never have the money to do? Don't be shy. Make a big list; live it up!

Now, next to each item you listed, write down the specific reason why you think you don't have the money for it. For example, let's say you answered that you've always wanted to rent a villa for a month in Tuscany. Perhaps the reason you don't have the money reads something like this: "I have one kid in college and one in private school. I don't make that kind of money."

Now I'd like you to revisit each reason you can't do what you've always wanted to do. Rewrite your responses with a positive thought. For example, instead of stating you don't make that kind of money, write something like: "I should look into payment options for next semester."

Here are some additional examples of negatives reframed as positives.

NEGATIVE	POSITIVE
I can't afford that.	I will start saving for that.
I don't know where to start.	I will create a plan.
I'll never get out of debt.	I choose to get out of debt.
This is just the way it is.	I know things will be different.
I don't make enough to save enough.	Every little bit of savings help.

Life is short. Focus on *can* instead of *can't*, *will* instead of *won't* and you'll be a lot closer to your ideal life.

A Grateful Heart

When I was at the height of my debt with sporadic income, my beloved "pimple on an elephant's ass" mentor, Bob Lyman, called me into his office one day to have a chat. He saw that I was letting my situation get the best of me. It was affecting my work too. He said that from that day forward, even weekends, I had to tell him five things I was grateful for, or else I'd be fired. It was official. I thought he was out of his mind. Still, I was playing the victim role really well those days, so it was easy for me to choose to be a victim of Bob's demand. In hindsight, I realize it was a simple and effective way to keep me focused on the positive. About a week later, Bob pulled me aside and said, "Murph, give me five." That day, I was feeling particularly cranky, defeated and ticked off, which of course he saw a mile away. Very ferociously, I said, "The birds, the bees, the flowers, the trees and the moon." I told him that I wasn't going to give him "the sun," which is the final part of the saying. He smiled at me and it made me laugh, so, in the end, he still got the sun. As little as this seems, teaching me to be grateful every day and to put those thoughts into words really did shift my consciousness to a more positive outlook. This was one of the greatest gifts I've ever received.

Grateful Moments

Journaling has become quite popular these days. I love the idea of keeping a "Gratitude Journal" as a place to record the gifts that life gives you on a daily basis. I don't know about you, but my days are so jam-packed that there are many evenings when I can't even remember if I ate lunch, let alone what I was grateful for! Sprinkling a little gratitude throughout my entire day works much better for me. I encourage you to give it a try. Say "thank you" for the little things that people do for you. Better yet, try to find something to be grateful for when you're in the midst of a bad situation. For instance, while you're stuck in traffic, be thankful that you have a car. If you arrive late to your destination, give thanks that you got there safely. By doing this you're recognizing the positive and giving it power. I think you'll find that the more positive experiences you give thanks for, the more positive experiences will come your way.

Who's afraid of change? That's an easy question to answer: pretty much everyone, especially when it comes to how we handle money. Most of us just aren't wired to alter our financial behavior easily. That's why the concept of setting your intentions to create change is difficult to embrace. Repeating the same patterns over and over again in life is quite natural. We gravitate to environments, feelings and personalities that are similar to those we've experienced before. This is true in every aspect of life, from relationships to career choices to how we handle our money. Stepping outside the familiar and changing our financial patterns isn't just difficult; it's downright scary. Our money is what I call a "warm and fuzzy." For the vast majority of people it's personal. We like to hold it close to our chests, keeping our financial affairs a private matter. After all, who wants to air their financial laundry in such a judgmental world?

Your Reality Can Change

I can't overemphasize my conviction that, the problem most often lies within our own perceptions. I'll never forget the first time I realized that things could be different. It was when I was twelve years old and my mom was pregnant with baby number eleven, later to be known as my little brother John Edward. For medical reasons, my mother had to go live with my grandparents for four months. From May until September, my Aunt Jeanne came to live at our house. Boy was life different! Aunt Jeanne's greatest strength is running a tight ship. She brought her organizational skills into our house that summer. It was the first time any of us had ever been on a schedule. We actually enjoyed it. I was in awe of her discipline and infatuated with the idea that life could be different from the one I had always known. The same thing happened to me when I went away to college. I was quite shocked to learn that not everyone was raised in a huge Irish Catholic family without a telephone!

The very idea of creating change in our lives can stir up such inner turmoil. We'd rather stay miserable or stay with the devil we know as opposed to the devil we don't, as the saying goes.

Mary's Story

Mary was blessed to be a member of the "Greatest Generation." Because of her frugal upbringing, she was reluctant to spend money on anything but life's necessities. This was a behavior she'd assumed early in life and she stuck to it like glue. As a result, by the time she was in her mid-sixties, Mary had amassed just under a million dollars in assets. Whenever I met with her to check in on her investments, she always mentioned that she really wanted a new kitchen. She'd had the same one since the '70s and felt it could really use an update. I'd say to her, "Mary, the interest on your assets is $34,000 a year. If you took just half of that, you'd have the best kitchen around!"

But Mary just couldn't bring herself to spend money on what she perceived to be such a luxury, particularly because her kitchen was still fully functioning the way it had been for years. After five years of working with her, I finally got her to take the plunge. She called me up one day and said, "I'm ready to do the kitchen." She told me she was going to spend around $17,000. Close to two years after she finished her kitchen, Mary died. Her passing saddened me on so many levels. Mary could have created her dream kitchen far earlier than she did and enjoyed it for many more years. What saddens me even more is that we as humans let our fears cause us to miss out on so many of life's pleasures. I truly believe that at the end of our days, our wealth is defined by the quality of the life we lived. So, what's your choice—to change or stay the same?

Quality of Life as Wealth

Wealth can be defined differently for different people. My mom would never define wealth as having a lot of money. She defines it as having all of her children around her for Sunday dinner and the money to provide that on a regular basis. Mom finds wealth in quality of life experiences with those she loves, so that is how her money flows.

The world is filled with people like my mom who believe that wealth isn't about having millions in the bank. It's about having enough to do the little things in life that truly make you happy. Here's what I find so fascinating about defining quality of life as wealth. If you do things that make you happy, like work in a career that you're absolutely passionate about, you will excel. Your opportunities will increase, your income will go up, and you will create abundance. I don't know about you, but this is certainly not what my professors taught in school. That model says you work, work, work and save, save, save and someday you can be happy. What's missing from that picture? It seems that someone forgot to tell them that all we have is the here and now. As I said earlier, in the Western world, this thought process is not supported because we're all trying to build wealth from the outside in, rather than from the inside out.

The Comfort of Repetition

I had a professor tell me once that the key to success in business is to occasionally step out of line, to be unpredictable. My basic nature is to keep things the same. I get nervous when I try something new or out of the ordinary. I purposefully try to put off things in my life that are new. As I said before, changing a behavior goes against our natural wiring. After all, we are animals who respond to behavioral conditioning.

A case in point: Let's say that you take a baby elephant and tie a rope around his leg (humanely, of course) and then secure the rope to a stake in the ground. The little elephant will soon realize that he isn't going anywhere. Now fast-forward in time, and the little elephant is fully grown and very strong. If you now tie a rope around his leg, he will immediately think he is staked to the ground and stand there all day, because his behavior was conditioned through years of being tethered to a stake. Question: Are you staked into the ground when it comes to how you handle money, conditioned by *your* past? Better yet, are you willing to take a step toward financial freedom? Are you ready to take those shackles off? If you are, I believe that you'll soon discover there is nothing holding you back. In order for your life to change, you have to believe that you have another option. Choosing something different for your life is like changing the TV channel. You're just tuning into a different frequency. The license plates on my car say CHOOZ 2 as a daily reminder to me and others how easily change can occur. It's our choice!

My License to Change

Let me explain to you how I came up with CHOOZ 2 for my license plates. During classes for my MBA at The University of Notre Dame, there was one week on campus called Integral Leadership. In preparation, we needed to have our co-workers at all levels fill out an evaluation on our performance as managers. This is known as a "360° Evaluation." I was scheduled to go over my evaluation with one of the business coaches and then create a personal and professional development plan to get me to the next level. As I was talking to this coach, he began asking me about my childhood. When I asked him why, he explained that people typically re-create the exact same dynamics in their work life that they experienced growing up. As the conversation continued, it became evident to me that I was conducting my adult life as if I were still Julie, the second oldest of twelve children, and that this was my identity, inside and out. Then I realized that as much as I tried to pull away from the pack and be my own person, I just never seemed to be able to succeed at it. I remained energetically and financially attached to my family by subsidizing my siblings and parents with cash, checks and other purchases (which was my deal, not theirs). I realized I needed to create a new reality.

My nickname has always been "Murph." As far back as I can remember, friends, family members, teammates—you name it—everyone called me Murph. By then, I had been married for two years and had taken my ex-husband's name, but I was still Murph. In fact, it had become so much of my identity that my license plates had read MURPH 12 for many years. I thought that was a fun symbol of my place in life, the second oldest of twelve kids. Many times my mom would say under her breath, "Gosh, I'd really like those license plates." One day I had an epiphany. MURPH 12 was meant for someone responsible for raising twelve children, and although my first "job" had been helping to raise ten, it was time for me to move on. To progress in my new reality as a financial professional, I needed to let go of my old identity. My mother was the one who had the twelve children, not me! That Christmas, I took the license plates off my car, wrapped them in a box and gave them to her. I've never seen someone so happy. I was stepping out of my mother's identity and she was fully stepping into her own. I then applied for new plates: CHOOZ 2. This was not only symbolic of my newfound right to choose to make some important changes in my life, but a very powerful claim for my future.

The Choice is Yours

What things are holding you back? What past identity are you holding onto? What beliefs define your behavior? Be aware of the language you use. Do you apologize a lot to other people? Do you shy away and say nothing? Are you playing the victim in your responses? Do you blame other people for your life? Take a look inward and examine what it is that you and only you can choose to change. These questions will lead you to information that can help you decide how you're going to live while moving forward. You are getting closer to designing what your future reality will be. Remember, your status in life is because of you, not anybody else's words or actions. The mere fact that you're reading this book demonstrates that you're open to change. From this day forward, I challenge you to keep your mind open to change and your heart open to the positive. You'll be amazed at what comes your way.

Lucky You

As strange as it may seem, part of your choice for a new financial reality revolves around choosing to be lucky. Sometimes I find it amusing that an industry driven by rational analysis would allow the notion of luck to factor into the equation. It's such a mystical concept, isn't it? An invisible force that strikes at random! Ooohhh! It sounds more like something out of a science fiction film than an everyday financial phenomenon. Still, the theory that good or bad fortune can happen to anyone, regardless of wealth or status, is alive and well, from the penthouse offices on Wall Street to the pits of the trading floor. Talk to any commodities or futures trader and they'll tell you they don't just believe in luck, it's practically their religion. It's easy to spot the lucky commodities traders. They're the superstitious ones who keep their personal money in cash or guaranteed bonds, not in the volatile and uncertain commodities market!

Remember the television commercial with old "Mrs. Fletcher" on the floor crying "Help! I've fallen and I can't get up!" The poor woman was all alone and no one was around to hear her. Then a spokesperson for a medical alarm service tells us about a necklace that can turn Mrs. Fletcher's predicament from bad to good luck. I believe that luck is a real phenomenon. Sure, it would have been lucky if Mrs. Fletcher's neighbor just happened to stop by, but a handy, waterproof alarm necklace that brings help when she needs it will position her to be "lucky." With good planning and preparation, you can beat the odds of bad luck, so to speak. What I'm saying is that you can actually set yourself up to be lucky—or at least to avoid many of the bad luck scenarios that in the financial arena can trap you in a cycle of struggling for survival.

Set Yourself Up for Success

Setting yourself up to be lucky can save you a lot of grumbling and complaining later on. We all know that the financial inevitabilities of life, from home repairs to taxes, are always right around the corner, but it's human nature to act surprised, dismayed or angry when they arrive.

You know that the awesome new SUV you just bought is going to require new tires someday, and at $250 a pop. Yet, when it comes time to pony up the bucks, you're resentful, right? Whether your home is modest or mansion-like, the roof will need replacing within ten years. Why let yourself get in a huff over it? Instead, plan for it. The high-speed toys or shiny, glitzy stuff that fascinate us are not going to last forever. Neither is your lovely home. Why not prepare yourself financially for the inevitable repairs or replacements? For example, so many homeowners are thrown for a loop when something major is in need of repair. Let's say the hot water tank goes kaput and suddenly you have a thousand dollar expense you didn't expect. Well, the reality of it is that things like this happen all the time. A hot water tank typically lasts seven to ten years. The last time I checked a new one costs around a thousand dollars. So if you take one thousand dollars over seven years, that means you need to save $142 per year (which is only $12 per month) in order to pay for the next one. If we all did this, and it's easy to do, then life's large expenses would never hit us where it hurts. Position yourself to be lucky. Open a savings account when you sign the lease on that new condo, and earmark the funds for inevitable expenses, like a surprise assessment or new carpeting. Create a fund for all the costs of owning a home. If, instead, you continue to allow yourself to play the victim, you'll always come from a mindset of scarcity.

I've always wanted a boat, so I started a Boat Fund. My current boat balance is about 7,000 bucks. I put a set amount in every month. Shortly, I'll buy my boat. Watching my boat fund grow is fun! I'm my own bank. I have a House Fund. I have a Murphy Relief Fund set up to help my brothers and sisters when they need it. I have a Real Estate Tax Fund. The best part is, because they are all electronic savings accounts, I earn interest on them while they grow. I also have an Annual Bills Fund so, for example, when my car insurance bill comes due every six months, I have the money. I also wind up paying less for the insurance because I pay it in a lump sum versus having a monthly surcharge added to the cost. Here's the best part: There's no mad scramble for cash. I just wire the money to my checking account and pay the bill. I'm still taking it out of my monthly flow, but in the meantime, I'm saving money by paying myself that interest. I'm in control. I even have a Christmas Fund that I start every January. During the months of the year when most people are nervous about paying for their holiday expenses, I'm funding mine for the following year.

The Autopilot Plan

We've all labeled situations in life as things that "just happened." Choose to not be a victim. Yes, life is full of surprises. My advice is to not dread those surprises, but do plan ahead and avoid as many as you can. Position yourself to be lucky and put those "surprise" expenses on autopilot. You can set it up just like your 401(k) and have the money come right out of your paycheck straight to the savings account. Remember, it's not how much money you make; it's what you do with the money you get.

Here's another way to position yourself for success. Once you've finished paying for your car, keep making the payments out of your cash flow, but pay yourself instead. This puts money straight into an account that's named for your intention. We all know that cars don't last forever, so why keep struggling with car payments and act like you never expected to have to buy a new one? Once the $400 monthly car payment is done, get the bank to put that same $400 per month from your cash flow automatically into a savings account to fund your next car. Don't leave it up to your own devices to put that money into savings. I'll say it again: *Position yourself to be lucky*. When it comes time to buy your next car, you still might have to take one-third to one-half of the car cost on the payment plan, but this time around you'll have a lower monthly payment. And maybe, if you choose to, you'll be able to pay all cash for the car the next time around. Become your own bank. It's empowering! People will probably look at you and think, "How did she do that?"

If you can't seem to get your spending under wraps and stick to a savings plan, here's something to try: Have your paycheck directly deposited into a savings account instead of checking. Then move over to checking only the amount you've decided you'll spend that month on all of your expenses. Most people call this a "budget." This will force you to go back to a cash basis, spending only what you have in cash, not in lines of credit, whether it's plastic or one of those "checks" the banks love to send you for a low interest rate (introductory, of course). Only 5% of Americans save first and then spend. These are the people who hold the most wealth in this country. Which side of the fence do you want to be on?

CHAPTER WRAP-UP

You have the power to change the course of your life. But first you must make a conscious choice to create a new reality.

Focus your intentions on what you want for your life, instead of wandering about blindly, waiting for things to change. A world of promise and possibilities will open up to you.

How you see yourself is how others see you. By choosing to think and speak positively, you invite more positive people and events into your life.

We all victimize ourselves with negative self-talk from time to time. Try to recognize when you're doing this and teach yourself to reframe your thoughts and words in a more positive way.

Some people judge wealth by how much money they have. I happen to believe wealth is a measure of the richness of our lives. It's possible to have a rich quality of life without being a millionaire. The key is allowing yourself to achieve the richness you desire.

Life is already full of surprises, especially financial ones. Instead of setting yourself up to be a victim; set yourself up to thrive. One way to do this is by setting aside money for the unexpected.

*"It is important to remember that we are energy...
And energy cannot be created or destroyed,
it just changes form."*

—Rhonda Byrne

5

YOUR TURNING POINT

I've found that in order to create a life of abundance, you must first define your ideal life. To do this, you must tune into your Inner Wealth. It will do you no good to listen to what I might think is your ideal life or anyone else's notion of happiness. This is about finding *your* ideal life. You're not going to stick with a plan unless it's your plan. It needs to resonate with you. A lot of folks in my industry just don't get this. They're intent on selling products based on cookie-cutter demographics and statistics, but those things don't really matter up front. These products come into play at the back end of the process, if at all.

Creating a Map for Change

I always love my first meeting with new clients. In the same way that attorneys employ a discovery process to prepare a case for litigation, I engage in a discovery interview to learn more about the people who have come to me for assistance. I explore each individual's financial history, examine current portfolios, learn more about why my clients chose the products they did, and uncover what has been their financial decision-making process. My absolute favorite part of the meeting begins about thirty minutes into the ninety-minute session. This is when we engage in a discussion about what makes them happy. I usually start with, "What does your ideal world look like?" or "What do you want your life to be like in the three to five years?" Inevitably, I hear, "You mean financially?" Or I get a funny look and crossed arms (the body language of protection). Once I explain that what I'm really asking for are their greatest desires in life, money aside, their demeanor softens—maybe not immediately. Some people enter my office with quite a bit of history, and it's usually not all good. Still, I am continually amazed at how even the biggest egos eventually do allow themselves to look past the pomp and power and gaze inward.

To me there is nothing more satisfying than helping someone step out from behind their social mask to reveal their hidden hopes, dreams, fears and aspirations. As difficult as it may be for some, looking inward is crucial to the quest for a life of abundance because what you want out of life eventually becomes the centerpiece of your personal financial plan.

Dreams and Your Life's Purpose

As a nation, we've forgotten how to dream. I find this sad, given that we live in a country where dreams can come true. Oh sure, society has made it easy for us to want things, but I'm talking about a higher level of dreams and desires. As I mentioned earlier, young people today have a strong sense of their own wishes and aspirations. I'm saying this as a social observation, not a judgment. Older siblings and parents, who are typically in their 30s, 40s and 50s, have learned how to have more cash inflow than generations past. What this has done is create a generation of young people who accept wealth as the status quo. They believe that everyone should have a cell phone, their own laptop, expensive vacations, designer clothes, etc. Time and time again, this has caused the younger generations to miss the foundation of what drove the cash in the first place—basic needs like food, clothing and shelter. Likewise, people in their 30s, 40s and 50s today have also forgotten this. We all know how to want things, but I believe we've forgotten how to desire loftier things, such as a living a life of quality, not quantity, which brings true happiness. The quality comes from living according to your life's purpose, your Inner Wealth.

Your life's purpose is a colorful mosaic of the many dreams you have for every aspect of your life. In Chapter One, where I talked about the Life Navigation Wheel, I pointed out that Western Culture has us functioning in a cycle of survival, by putting work or money at the center of the wheel. When we do this, we're perpetually scraping and saving to maintain a certain lifestyle or achieve a better "someday." Now I'd like you to start thinking of your wheel as having your life's purpose, or Inner Wealth, at the center, with the other four circles surrounding it. When you do this, you shift your focus away from money. Instead, you're motivated by what you want out of life. This is the foundation for a life of thriving.

I often ask clients what they think they're great at. For some folks this is a very easy question; for others, it can be a real stumper. Knowing what you're great at in life is clearly linked to your life's purpose. I asked you earlier to think of a time when you were doing something and all of a sudden time seemed to have flown by. Moments like these are created when you're tuned into your soul's desire. It creates a wonderful harmony in your life. If the feeling of time flying by doesn't happen to you at work, clearly you need to evaluate your work life and make a change. If it's not happening at home, some kind of shift has to happen there. If it's not happening for you personally, there's a change in balance that needs to occur in your everyday life.

Beth's Story

Beth came to me years ago because she felt a gap between her current reality and what she really wanted to be doing for a living. For over 30 years, she had been a registered nurse. When she came to me, she was in her early sixties and her body wasn't handling the long hours spent on her feet as well as it used to. Beth realized she had a passion that she'd tapped into on occasion throughout her working years; she absolutely loved to write. She'd been writing screenplays for nearly a decade and some had even found their way to interested producers in L.A. One day, she called to tell me that she was ready to follow her heart. We immediately set up a plan for her. She's currently in transition between her old life and her new adventure. As revenues are coming in from her scripts, she's cutting back on her hours at the hospital. Beth is truly following her passion— and getting paid for it.

I can honestly say that since I've come to understand my life's purpose and am living with that as the center of my existence, I will choose not have any regrets when it comes time for my physical body to leave this earth. I challenge you to stake the same claim.

Making a List of Your Dreams

A couple of years ago, a friend kept going on and on that he felt unfulfilled. He began obsessing over his perception that I'd already done so much in my life by the ripe old age of twenty-eight, while he had done nothing. One day, he kept complaining about this as we were driving back from a "Fighting Illini" basketball game down in Champaign, and I felt like I was listening to a broken record. He just couldn't get past his feelings of inadequacy and shame. I decided it was time for him to make his list—the list of what he had dreamed of doing since he was a kid. As he drove, I pulled out a piece of scrap paper and said, "Okay, time to make your dream list." Soon he had included all kinds of great things on his list. He wanted to attend a Notre Dame football game, go to a Big Ten football game, use his vacation days to actually leave town, go to Europe, travel to see another major league baseball stadium outside Chicago, go to a Chicago Bears game, and much more.

It was interesting to me that all these things, which seemed pretty easy to do, were monumental tasks for him. He never thought he could reach out and grab each and every one of them. But he did. Over the following year he went down his list and knocked off each desire, one at a time. I was amazed at how excited he became when the stress of those unfulfilled dreams was lifted from his shoulders and he could enjoy life again. The exercise helped him do things that moved his soul. When his first list was completed, he began to tackle other life dreams. It's sad how many people go through life without pursuing their passions—big or small—or forego actions that make them giggle. It isn't hard; we just have the perception that it is unobtainable. I find many people start small. As you find yourself achieving the little things, bigger dreams start to seem more within reach. And, living your dreams yields a life of no regrets—unquestionably one of the greatest characteristics of an abundant and rewarding life.

I've decided the boat I'm dreaming about owning is going to be named Dare 2 Dream. I'm ready to catch the wave!

I invite you to make a list like my friend did. Stop and ponder the things you've always wanted to do. Feel the excitement welling up inside as you write them down. They're all there for the taking. Come on, grab them! When you're done, give yourself a timeline to actually accomplish everything on your list— six months, a year, five years. It doesn't matter. It's your list, and it's time to bring it on!

Your Dream Life

In a moment, I'm going to have you brainstorm about your ideal life. Forget about being realistic. This is your opportunity to dream. No one's going to read what you've written unless you let them; they're your private thoughts. We all have responsibilities in this world, and we'll get to those at hand, but right now it's really important that you just dream about the ideal. What you want doesn't even have to make sense. It's important to just set the intention of what you want to attract into your life. Many of us get hung up on how that will show up, but life works in mysterious ways, allow the mystery and allow the universe to deliver your dreams. They never come in exactly how you thought they would come about, but they will come. Your job is to hold the intention and don't veer from it.

Money Isn't the Answer

The rest of this chapter is going to be a series of exercises to help you begin to think in terms of what you want out of life. What is your soul yearning for? What do you truly desire? Please don't say millions of dollars. You may think that's all you really need or want in life and that if you had Donald Trump's net worth, everything would be hunky dory. Stating money as the answer is hardly scratching the surface. Financial wealth may be our source of leverage to get things in our world today, but if the entire financial structure were to fall apart, what would you do? Of course you need to set financial goals or desires you'd like to achieve, but creating a life of abundance is about so much more than that.

To this day, my dad believes that if he had money all his problems would go away. Trust me, I've met enough millionaires to know that having it all is never enough. I can't get over the fact that we all know how to want *things*. Society has made that part easy. But we're not used to wanting in the bigger picture. When immigrants first came to this country, they truly desired better lives for themselves and their families. They came to America to make their dreams come true. Our society has lost that urgent incentive. I know the concept of reaching for your dreams can be difficult to comprehend, but join me. Join me in the stratosphere for a moment and consider lofty notions such as the values you hold dear—for example happiness, peace, pure bliss. Dream of what it is that you'd like to see happen in your life, no matter how wacky it may seem. Think about it from every possible angle. Be sure to be authentic in your responses. Sure you have responsibilities in this world, as we all do, and we'll get to this shortly, as I said. But for right now it's really important that you dream about your ideal world.

13 EXERCISE

Life Transformation Exercise

Remember the illustration of your Life Navigation Wheel from Chapter One? You're now ready to tune in to your Inner Wealth and create a wheel of your own. You'll need pencil and paper and a quiet place to sit.

The first thing I'd like you to do is sit quietly. Breathe deeply and listen to the beat of your heart. Follow its rhythm. Feel its strength. Picture yourself sitting with your eyes closed, face upward to the sun. Drink in the warmth and heat. Absorb it into every pore. Follow the warmth through your limbs, into your core. Feel the energy and power of your true self. Think about the values and principles you stand for. Consider the things that are important to you. Ponder your special gifts and abilities. Take a few more deep breaths and open your eyes.

Take out your paper and pencil and draw a center circle for your Inner Wealth (see Figure 5 below). It doesn't matter if it looks like an amoeba—your drawing isn't being judged. Then draw four circles surrounding your center and label them as they are in the diagram: Work Life, Family Life, Personal Life, and Financial Life. You're now ready to begin.

Figure 5

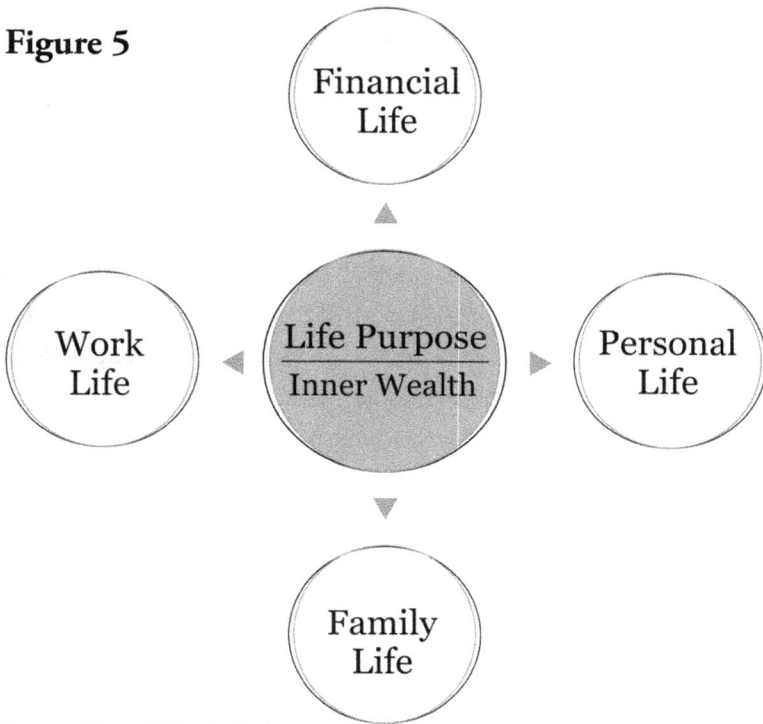

Part One—Your Work Life

People tend to be very clear about whether or not they love their jobs, so it's a great place to start. If you love your job, please move on to the next category. If not, please continue reading. Examine each of the questions below. Sit with each one for a moment. Open your mind to all of the possibilities that are out there.

- ✓ What do you *really* want to be doing as your livelihood?
- ✓ What type of work wouldn't even seem like work to you?
- ✓ What is it about your job that causes you stress or pleasure?
- ✓ What is it about your current employer or employees that ruffle your feathers?
- ✓ Do you dream of working for yourself?
- ✓ What do others say you're really great at?
- ✓ What do others say you should have been?

14   EXERCISE

Work Life Exercise

Now I'd like you to picture yourself doing something you truly love. Go ahead, put the book down for a moment and create a scene in your head. Imagine that you're getting paid for it. Actually picture yourself at the bank depositing the income from your business or looking at that paycheck from the job you love. Feel the satisfaction and gratitude in your heart that comes from knowing you're financially rewarded for doing what you do best.

When you're ready, refer back to the blank Life Navigation Wheel that you just drew. Next to the circle named Work Life, I'd like you to write down how you see your ideal. Picture it in your mind. Be as descriptive and detailed as you like.

Love It or Leave It?

Few people I meet are in love with what they do for a living. Typically they're still in their current job because they have other commitments, things like family, debts or lifestyle choices, that keep them there, that is not ideal.

Much of Corporate America is out of touch with their employees' need to have a better overall quality of life. Too many people are working too many hours. The cover of *Crain's Chicago Business Magazine* caught my eye the other day. It featured an article about corporate waste, and reported that companies with more than 20,000 employees experience much higher claim rates on their health insurance. People are breaking down and something has got to give. In the long run, we can't continue at this pace, especially those who don't love their jobs. I have now owned my own business for several years, and there are some weeks I work 60-70 hours. That doesn't happen often, but when it does, it isn't stressful, because I love what I'm doing. At the same time, I've come to a point in my life where I deserve to nurture my body and soul and keep everything in harmony, and since you are reading this—clearly so have you.

Another thing to keep in mind is that you may have loved your job in the past, people change. Perhaps the same things don't motivate you as they did in the past. It's okay to say you want to do something different. It just takes courage to take a stand for what you want and create a game plan for making that your new reality.

What's the Right Job for You?

I work with many business owners, and I find that there's often ongoing tension between employer and employees. Employers know what jobs need to be done, and these may or may not be within the skill sets of the employees they've hired to do them. In my opinion, it's really important to have every employee do what they absolutely love doing every day, ideally something they're passionate about. People whose skill sets match their employer's needs are the golden ticket to success. Everybody wins, because both the employee and the company can thrive. When we perform tasks that are outside of our current passions, things begin to deteriorate because we grow stagnant. All of us spend too much time in our work life to *not* love it!

I've created a list that I use with new hires. I've also used it with many clients. It's in the back under Appendix 1. Basically, it consists of a list of job functions. If you'd like some help in determining if a job is right for you—or if an employee is right for a certain job—go to the back of the book and follow the instructions. It should give you some clarity as to what you're looking for in a new hire, a new position, or even a new career. You may have started your current job because you were passionate about it at one time, but you've grown to a new place. People who choose to stay in a function they are not passionate about typically wind up miserable. They keep the job for reasons that don't excite them, that don't feed their soul. I don't care how old you are, it's never too late to do what you absolutely love.

Part Two—Your Family Life

Again, consider each of these questions carefully, as you begin to imagine your ideal family life.

✓ Are your friends your family?

✓ Do you long to spend more time with your kids, or nieces and nephews?

✓ Do you desire more time alone with your partner or spouse?

✓ Do you desire to have a partner or spouse?

✓ What hobbies or activities do you do together as a family?

✓ Are you ready to get married and start a family?

✓ Do you want to have a child despite not being married?

✓ Would you prefer to be a family with one income versus two, in order to have one spouse raise your children?

✓ Do you long to escape a bad relationship that's not feeding your soul?

✓ What values do you desire to instill in your marriage and the lives of your children?

Now, on your wheel, next to the Family Life circle, record your ideal family life. Write it exactly as you want it to look, down to the last detail.

The Family Foundation

As much as I would like to ignore them, I have to bring up the Joneses again. I think one of the biggest challenges for us as a society today is the need to redirect our focus away from envying what everyone else has, and consider what we can do for each other. We've lost what was once the foundation of family and community life in America—trust, equality, freedom, well-being. Yes, times have changed, but from an emotional standpoint, people still hunger to be a part of something greater than themselves. Children today are seeking a family foundation. If they don't naturally have it, they'll create it, whether it's through friends or in other ways, both positive and negative. They'll be drawn to whoever or whatever will fulfill their souls' desires.

It still amazes me when I remember that even though we didn't have much money, we were the most popular family on the block. After school and on weekends, the neighborhood kids would flock to our yard or through the front door of our house. There was one family whose five children were at our house constantly. Both of their parents worked full time. They must have been searching for the love and affection that their parents, who weren't home due to work constraints, couldn't give them. I was very fortunate to have a mother who stayed home with all of us, even though she had her hands full—and then some.

These days there are many positive things about having a parent at home with the children. There are positive aspects to daycare as well, such as the exposure to group interaction and educational resources that help prepare little ones for success in school. The beauty is that the choice is yours to make. So what will it be?

Gina's Story

Gina was a woman so eager to start a family that she got pregnant on her honeymoon. Nine months later she gave birth to twins. I met Gina and her husband when the twins were four years old. Needless to say, they were eager to get started on their financial plan. At the time they could only save about $150 per month. It's not a lot of money, but directionally it was correct. A couple years later they had another child. By then, Gina really wanted to stay home with all three kids. She brought in $45,000 annually for the household, which was 48% of their household income. Over a period of three years, we slowly shifted their lifestyle to reduce debt and expenses and to save any pay increases each of them received. We made a plan to save more and more of her paycheck, until finally they were able to rely on her husband's income exclusively. I'm happy to report that she's been able to stay at home caring for their now four children for the past four years and is definitely living the life she desired.

What is a Family Anyway?

What if you don't have children? What if you're an only child? What if you have a very small family or no family at all? These days, "family" is not necessarily defined as having blood relatives. Your family can be people you love and with whom you share a spiritual bond. If you're single, do you want to adopt a child? Do you want to get married? I suspect that many people who want to be married are not yet because they're not whole within themselves, which makes attracting a partner more difficult. It's just something to think about. Perhaps your life purpose is to help others without being a parent or spouse. Teachers and people in volunteer organizations often give life-changing assistance to children whose parents are unable to. Whatever your story, the key is to dream about your family life the way you want it to be. It's the only life you have, and you deserve to make the best of it.

Part Three—Your Personal Life

It's time to focus on you and you alone, your health, hobbies and overall wellbeing.

- ✓ Do you wish you could do more for your overall health?
- ✓ Are you feeling overweight, out of shape or chronically tired?
- ✓ Is travel one of the most important things in the world to you?
- ✓ What life goals have you yet to fulfill?
- ✓ Is there a hobby, sport or activity that you've always wanted to try?
- ✓ Do you dream of running in a marathon?
- ✓ Do you long to disappear for a while to write a book?

Once you have pondered your answers to these questions, return to your wheel and write down your ideal Personal Life. Include goals, challenges, achievements—whatever excites you.

Your Body

It's all over the media that Americans are growing more overweight by the day. We can point the finger at many different reasons. One thing is for certain— that personal health has not been a priority for the majority of U.S. citizens in recent decades. But, without our health, we have nothing. Why is it that our health is so commonly the last thing we focus on? What type of body do you dream of? I'm certainly not telling you to go out and get plastic surgery. What I'm saying is that it's time to look at the details. How do you want your teeth to look? Maybe you smoke and you don't like the fact that your teeth are yellow. Do you want better skin? Do you wish you could eat more healthfully? Remember, permanent change only occurs if you heal from the inside out, not from the outside in, just like your financials!

Hobbies and Interests

Another way of thinking about your personal life is to examine how you would ideally like to spend your time outside of family, work or money commitments. Ladies, this is an area I see where we get in our own way. We give up so much of ourselves to others that we forget about ourselves. Then we get angry at our partners or spouses when they want to go out with their buddies. The reality is that we're not feeding our own soul's desires, and we tend to look externally in order to blame someone else for not nurturing ourselves. Some things to consider are spending time with friends, playing sports, singing, dancing, playing an instrument, traveling, going to the beach, furthering your education formally or not—doing things that feed your soul, not for anyone else, just for you. Do you want to do things that aren't necessarily about achievement or completing a task? Maybe you want to shift from *doing* to *being* by creating a more balanced or harmonic life. What would you like to make more of as a priority in your life

Part Four—Your Financial Life

This is where you begin designing your future. Don't hold back. Be honest with yourself as you consider these questions. And remember, no negative self-talk allowed!

- ✓ What financial life do you dream of?
- ✓ Are you seeking financial independence?
- ✓ Do you want to get a handle on your cash flow?
- ✓ Do you want to reduce your financial commitments to others?
- ✓ At what age do you wish to stop working (retire)?
- ✓ Do you dream of being massively generous to those less fortunate than you?
- ✓ Do you have anything that you want to acquire (like the way I want my boat)?

Building Wealth from the Inside Out

As odd as it may seem, this is one of the areas I like to call the "warm and fuzzies" because I believe your financial life is directly linked to your heart. Sure, most people aren't comfortable with opening up about their finances. The world around us has deluded us into believing that personal power is achieved through financial gain, but as you've heard me say several times, to me this is the complete opposite of the truth. If you retain your personal power and stay true to who you are according to your Life's Purpose, your life will be overflowing with money.

I encourage you to think outside the box here. I have a couple of clients who chose to build enough assets to allow them to earn about half of their regular salary from investments, thus improving their quality of life by working only part-time. I have other clients who aligned themselves with forward—thinking employers. Their companies offer a reduced salary in exchange for more personal time or long-term sabbaticals. There are many options out there if you dare to be creative.

What type of accumulation goals do you have, and what specifically are you doing to fulfill them? I have a friend who wants to purchase a house in the city of Chicago. The asking price is about one million dollars. At my suggestion, she opened a savings account that is named "House," with the address of the house she wants to buy. That's pretty specific! Thanks to the Law of Attraction I discussed earlier, she is definitely moving even closer to getting her dream house.

Do you dream of being able to provide a college education for your children? For some people their dream is to support various charities, and it's actually quite easy to create your own foundation. It might seem funny but anyone can. So, it's all up to you. Just keep those juices flowing. As I've said before and will keep repeating, I'm here to help you make financial choices based on who *you* are and where *you* want to go. But this is a two-way street. Documenting your dreams is the first step toward achieving those personal goals.

Transition Points

If you're single and about to be married, this is a transition point in your life. Moving from no kids to your first child is another one. Transitioning from working to retirement years is another big crossroad. Transition points in life occur between the many stages of modern living, and at those junctures it's crucial that you redefine your life's purpose. The majority of baby boomers are currently collectively facing a transition point in their lives. The kids are gone, college tuition is paid, and baby boomers are getting the biggest pay raise of their lives. They're not ready to stop working yet. What are they going to do during their thirty years plus of retirement? They've watched their parent's age rapidly after retiring. Quite often, people who don't know what to do with themselves during this time in their lives are the ones who become ill and die shortly after they retire. If you're at the older end of the boomer generation, think about what you want this next phase of your life to be like. Find a compelling reason to keep on living, not dying. Is it more travel? Is it starting to work less while still keeping your mind engaged? Do you want to spend more time with the grandkids? Do you want to move? What is it? Begin to define yourself for the next three decades to come. If you're about to have a child, visualize what you want your new family life to look like. Will both parents continue to work, or will one parent stay home? It's much easier to create a plan *before* the baby arrives than after.

15 EXERCISE

Life Stages Visualization Exercise

Now, take another break from reading and visualize your life from the perspective of life stages. Have fun with it, go crazy, be creative—but by all means be positive. What you visualize is exactly what you'll manifest! If it helps, cut out pictures that illustrate your ideal life. Or if you're talented like my sisters Marianne and Katie, draw your ideal world. Remember, thoughts become facts. The energy you put out attracts like energy. Think of it as meeting someone for the first time, when you get a good or bad feeling about them. If it's bad energy that you interpret, you probably don't have much in common with this person. Trust your intuition. Sense that energetic pull. No matter what, don't waste another minute of your life wondering if you'll have enough money to live your dreams. State your intentions for your money clearly and positively. Follow the guidelines in the next few chapters and you will manifest your dreams!

Your Financial Turning Point

If you've completed the exercises in this book thus far, you've just arrived at an important milestone in your journey toward abundance. You have reached your financial turning point. You're now separated from the pack. You're poised to build your wealth in order to achieve the life that you want for you and your family, today and in the future!

The money you currently earn and have in the bank, your investments, real estate, retirement funds—the whole kit and caboodle—is going to have a new purpose, many new purposes in fact, all based on your intentions. You'll soon be able to apportion your funds effectively to realize those intentions. In just a few more chapters you will have a greater ability to build wealth and realize the lifestyle you want to have for yourself and your family, now and for the rest of your lives. If you were to choose to stay in survival mode, you'd be among the unfortunate majority who believe they must work for 15 to 20 years to achieve their millions so that they can then live on 5% of their net worth a year in retirement. I don't have to tell you that the pressure that comes with that kind of thinking is excruciating. What if you lose your job or become ill? If you're not funding the life that you want, you're heading for misery, alcoholism or both. However, if you're living your life's purpose and apportioning your money according to your desired intentions, you have set yourself up to be lucky, and abundance can be yours.

CHAPTER WRAP-UP

An important step on your journey to happiness and abundance is to define your ideal life from every aspect. How you define it is by recognizing your dreams.

As a country, we've forgotten how to dream. How ironic is it that the dream for a better life is how this great country came about!

You cannot progress from surviving to thriving without acknowledging your ideal life and creating a plan to realize those ideals.

The world around us teaches that power is achieved through financial gain. I believe the opposite is true—that if you retain your personal power and live your life focused on your true self, your life will be overflowing with money.

"You are afraid of your own empowerment as much as those around you are afraid of your becoming empowered."

—Caroline Myss

THE CRABS IN YOUR BUCKET

As you begin to listen to your Inner Wealth and take steps to follow your heart's desires, something may begin to change in your relationships with others. You may find that the people you've been the closest to in your life have suddenly began to pull away. There's a good chance you may no longer share the same emotional or physical bonds that were once so similar. This is quite common among recovering alcoholics or drug addicts. Those who make sweeping changes in personal behavior also undergo interpersonal shifts. Simply put, the people who enable you in your current financial reality may not be your best pals once you choose to change. Please don't allow yourself to become disheartened by this. I promise you, any friend or family member whose approval or affection you may lose as a result of following your life's purpose will be replaced tenfold—if not in number, in quality.

The Fighting Irish

What's with the reference to crabs? I'll explain with a story. Since the day I came out of the womb, I was told about The University of Notre Dame. My grandfather, Donald Anthony Murphy, played football there in the 1940s. He was a family legend. Unfortunately, I never met him. He died in 1964. My father, Donald Thomas, has always bled blue and gold from every pore. He's what The Fighting Irish folks call "subway alumni," a huge fan who never went to school there. As kids, we were taught the Notre Dame Fight Song even before we learned how to sing our ABCs. I can even play it on the piano—and I never took piano lessons.

Mom used to tell us stories about her dating years with Dad. They frequently traveled to South Bend on game days without any tickets, hoping to get in. Somehow my dad always came through. I'm not sure who was more amazed by his good fortune at finagling cheap tickets, Mom or Dad! Today I'd explain their good fortune as the Law of Attraction or karma at work.

Given all this, it made total sense to me that when I was ready for college, I'd go to Notre Dame, and this assumption caused me a great deal of conflict. Since everybody loved Notre Dame so much, I couldn't believe how many neighbors, friends and other locals were totally unsupportive. I must have heard a million times that kids like me didn't go to Notre Dame. We were the South-Side Irish of Chicago, and poor kids don't go to Notre Dame. Folks like us are just fans of the school team. Even my dad said, "Julie, you can't go there because we can't afford to send you. Only rich kids go to Notre Dame!" I've always regretted that I listened to all those people. I never even applied to get in… until I went there for my MBA!

The Crabs Pull You Down

Those negative family members, friends and neighbors were the "crabs in my bucket." Every time I wanted to escape my place in life, they'd reach up and pull me back into the bucket with them. If you've ever been to the shore and seen how live crabs behave in a bucket, you know exactly where the metaphor comes from. If you put one crab in a bucket, it can climb out by itself, no problem. But if you fill the bucket with twenty crabs, just as one gets to the rim, the other crabs pull it back down.

I have my mentor, Bob Lyman, to thank for the expression. Because of my Irish background, I've heard an awful lot of references to taverns. Most of them are quite inane, but I find Bob's axiom of life true in many ways. He explained to me that once you follow a new path in life, you can't go back and "sit on the same barstool" because you'll no longer see things in the same way as your old cronies. Putting it bluntly, the people from your past become like crabs in a bucket. They'll pull you back into your old ways.

My Crabs, the Early Years

Throughout my school years I was an active kid. I played softball, delivered the paper, and later worked at the local pizza joint. I was always a little pudgy but I just figured I was a bigger girl. When I was in high school, my body image issues didn't just come to life, they set up camp in my mind where they could pick at me day and night. One afternoon I was wearing one of those groovy V-neck sweaters that required a collared shirt underneath. My sweater was yellow and my blouse was black and white. I walked into the lunchroom one day, and a guy I didn't even know came up to me and said, "Hey, look at the giant banana."

That was it. I stopped eating. I swear I didn't eat anything for about six months, except every other Friday when I'd allow myself two breadsticks (the little crusty ones that come in packs) and one pizza puff per month. I was playing spring softball, and one afternoon I passed out from hunger on third base. I didn't care about my health. All I wanted was no one calling me a fat banana ever again. Sometimes I'd let myself eat two breadsticks for lunch *and* dinner. Wow, talk about living on the edge. Eventually I graduated to a couple of chicken sandwiches from Wendy's each week. By the time I went to college, between the fasting and all my campus activities, I'd become quite svelte and men began to pay attention to me. I had no idea how to deal with this, since the main attention I'd drawn previously was as the literal butt of a fat joke!

Hometown Pain

Although my body was now athletic and trim, in my mind I was still overweight, and this was the cause of tremendous insecurity. Consequently, when I returned to Chicago after graduation, the crabs in my bucket, made up of family, friends and neighbors, had a field day. People I'd grown up with and been around all of my life called me a traitor. They claimed that I'd forsaken my South-Side identity for North-Side snobbery. I was driving a new Honda Accord, and I remember thinking, "It's not a Mercedes." But to them, it was fancy, and that meant I no longer belonged. They could no longer identify with me, and that made them feel vulnerable—all because I'd lost weight, earned a college degree and bought a brand new car that wasn't a "beater," and—worst of all—I lived downtown!

Well, once again, unconsciously, I yielded to my bucket of crabs and believed what they said. I had no place masquerading as an attractive, smart and fit young woman. Within a few years, the weight came back, pound by pound, until I weighed more than I ever had in my entire life. I made the "fat banana" of my high school days look like Olive Oyl. Darn crabs and silly me for letting them control my personal power.

Crab Empathy

Over time I've come to realize that when you alter your course in life, many people who are closest to you feel vulnerable and uneasy. It's a reality of life; when people decide to change, those around them often don't like it. They'll unconsciously try to get you back to your old behavior. This is because when you start down another path, and others sense you're moving on, they feel threatened. It forces them to look at their own lives, and they may not be ready to do so. I've always said that people come and go in our lives for reasons. Some are meant to stay and others are not. It's human nature for those feeling left behind to badmouth or ridicule you, rather than wish you well. Those buddies who've taken up residence at the bar, health club, salon or the neighbor's kitchen are not bad people. They're just functioning on a different frequency from the new you. It's not your place to judge them, but do recognize that they're on a different path. If you want to explore new territory, you're going to have to wish them well on their journey, even if it doesn't include you. I used to let my crabs get the best of me. Their behavior triggered tremendous feelings of intolerance and impatience, which was irritating to me. I soon realized that I didn't need to develop more tolerance or patience for them. I needed to focus on my goals and dreams and move on. Which I did!

Ayurvedic Connection

Chapter Two touched on the chakras of the body and the waste that can accumulate from toxic emotions. There is a holistic form of medicine, one that originated in India thousands of years ago, called Ayurveda or Ayurvedic Medicine. Among the many fascinating aspects of this unique approach to wellness and healing is the concept that our bodies must be in a state of equilibrium or harmony with our true selves in order to achieve total health. An Ayurvedic physician sees each person as totally different and separate from the next. As you're reading these words, you have your own unique energy coursing through your body, dictating your physical and emotional balance. If, for example, you just ate a snack that is not in alignment with your energy flow (which for me would be a big bowl of pasta) your body will not process that food properly. This will cause a buildup of toxic particles in various zones of your body. This toxic buildup is called *ama,* and, over time, it will collect in a vulnerable area and eventually result in disease.

What on earth does this have to do with your financial health? I find this a wonderful parallel with your financial health. When you're not living a life aligned with your life's purpose, the obstacles or crabs around you create a negative buildup, a financial *ama* if you will, which will eventually cause a blockage to your success. This is why you must take steps to rid yourself of the people and things that stand in your way.

What is keeping you off track?

Some of the obstacles that can appear as crabs in your bucket are time, money, debt levels and interest rates, and financial jargon.

Time

These days it's easy to feel like the time-challenged rabbit in *Alice in Wonderland.* We're all running to and fro, complaining about how late we are and how little time we have—yet we all have the same 24/7. Isn't it peculiar that something as nebulous as time has such a stronghold on the civilized world? For many of us, it seems like there's hardly a minute in the day to eat or rest, let alone balance the checkbook, right? Well, part of what's so appealing about the wealth-building process I recommend is that once you're up and running, it requires little time and effort on your part. I've also found tremendous value in making time for meditation. Interestingly enough, the more time I devote to it, the calmer I am. This, in turn, makes me more productive, leaving me more free moments throughout my day. Keep in mind though, that meditation can be many things to many people. Meditation can be running on a treadmill; it can be talking a walk around the neighborhood, watching the sunset, praying or using a mantra. All it really means is taking time to calm your mind so you can connect with your soul. Soaking in a bubble bath with no distractions can also work!

Money/Cash Flow

Think back to a time when you earned very little income. Remember how it seemed like you pinched every penny, but there still wasn't ever enough? I'm going to bet that you probably feel pretty close to that today, despite the fact that you make much more money. It has become second nature to increase our standard of living in proportion to our income. The biggest challenge I see here is that if you continually increase your spending, and you don't increase your savings level, at some point in your life you'll have to decrease your lifestyle. You'll have to live in retirement at a lower level of income than you were in the decade before you left the workforce.

Many people have said to me that once they retire, their house will be paid off, the kids will be on their own, and they won't need as much money in retirement. The reality I've experienced is that, yes, most people do have more disposable income after they pay off their homes and their children grow up and leave. What many clients fail to realize, however, is that they are still going to need a substantial income, because they want to travel more, spend more on grandkids, etc. And that doesn't even factor in inflation. Plus, if you're not working, what will you do to fill your time? In most cases, retired people don't spend less money; they just shift what they're spending their money on. That being said, there are plenty of ways to create some wiggle room with your cash flow. We'll get to that shortly.

Debt Levels and Interest Rates

It's amazing to me how easily we become comfortable with something the longer we're exposed to it. Debt is certainly one of those things. If you look at anyone who lived through the Great Depression, they're extremely sensitive to debt. It's not hard to figure out why. People who lived through the Depression had to learn to live on a shoestring, a concept most of us today cannot even fathom. Having debt puts you on the hook for *having* to work. You have a responsibility to go to work and pay that debt down until it's paid in full. This causes you to put money in the spotlight, along with how many hours you work, how much you make, how hard it is to get ahead, etc. To make matters worse, even if anything out of the ordinary occurs in your life, you will still need to go to work to pay your debts. It's a dangerous trap.

Then there's the issue of the interest rates you're paying on your debts. If you're going to carry debt, take a look at what you're actually paying out for it. It's amazing how by altering the little pieces you can improve the bigger picture. As interest rates have increased over the past couple of years, many people have found themselves in a real cash flow crunch, because their interest rates were variable instead of fixed. I know far too many folks whose payments are now triple what they used to be.

You're Not an Expert and You Don't Speak Finance

Many people are not aware that 401(k) investment plans for retirement came into existence in the early '80s. Before this, only people with large amounts of money actually invested in the stock market. Since then, most Americans have become at least somewhat familiar with what a mutual fund is, since it's the vehicle used in most 401(k) plans. Here's an interesting tidbit: When the markets declined in 2000, 2001, and 2002, the most common lawsuits against employers were claims about the lack of education on 401(k) plans. Employees claimed they were not up to speed with how those types of investments moved over time, and chose to blame someone else for not allocating their investments properly. In a number of companies, the employer will now have a financial professional come in to educate staff members on their 401(k) money. But what about becoming better informed about the rest of your financial world?

I was not brought up with money, but I am blessed to have learned how to grow wealth for myself and for others, because I know both sides of the coin, so to speak. Now, I can converse in two languages, English and financial jargon. Financial jargon is that gibberish-speak financial folks use when talking about their products and services, numbers, rates, percentages and the like. Not understanding your financial advisor is a big hurdle to get over, no matter how much or how little money you have. This is a perfect example of a crab you have no control over whatsoever—unless you have a translator handy.

Another common obstacle is all of the options that are available to you: investments, savings, insurance, etc. I find it easier to categorize financial products according to your needs. I break them down into buckets. You have short-term, mid-term and long-term buckets to put your money in. I'll get into more detail about this in Chapter Eight. What's important for you to understand right now is that the myriad financial products that are out there don't have to be as mystifying as they're made out to be. Again, it's important that you work with a financial professional who translates financial-speak into terminology you can identify with. You don't want someone to make your eyes glaze over when it comes to chatting about your financials.

Misperceptions about Viable Options

When I first got into the industry, to get a professionally managed account you had to have over a million dollars. Today, with retail fund accounts, you can get in with as little as $50 per month. Most people I encounter who have yet to plan for their future, or have done so minimally, think they have to have some large sum of money. Ladies and gentlemen, I'm here to tell you that this is not the case. You can accomplish pretty much anything you want to do. The industry has become very flexible, and it can accommodate almost any net worth these days. Who cares if you have to start small? At least we live in a country that makes it relatively easy to start at all!

Now for those of you who have been building your wealth for years, I've found you have a different challenge. The majority of people in this great country of ours have been doing business with financial professionals who don't have access to a full array of investment options. This is where you can really experience misperceptions about what's available and what's best for you. I can't tell you how many extremely wealthy men and women I meet have spent years with a stockbroker, only to wake up and suddenly yearn for something more. They're seeking a professional relationship that gives them more than just specific stocks and bonds recommendations. Their risk tolerance has changed and they've become interested in more than simply stocks and bonds, but they're not being informed about all that's available to them. Research done by Ibbotson Associates, a leading authority on asset allocation with expertise in capital market expectations and portfolio implementation, showed that 91.5% of performance of an investment portfolio is based on how well you diversify your assets. One great way to diversify is to have investment holdings outside the stock and bond markets. I read an article recently that said that if you had $100 million, you could invest in a specific portfolio built with privately held companies. Talk about options! You may not have this one, nor do many people have a spare $100 million sitting around, but most can still be more diversified.

Here's another misperception: Real estate is not a viable investment for everyday people. Perhaps people you know aren't willing to take the risk of investing in real estate. What about rental property or commercial leasing? It ties up funds, but does that lack of liquidity fit with your risk tolerance? There are many options to get into real estate. They can be great investment alternatives to consider. For instance, even non-traded real estate investment trusts (REITs) or limited partnerships can perform exceptionally well. You do need to make sure you're an informed investor, and make sure your investments match your personal risk tolerance. As you can see, your options may not be as limited as you perceive.

Fear of Risk or Addiction to Risk

In trying to educate people about their retirement plans, many financial firms have come up with targeted portfolios based almost exclusively on age. For example, if you're 40 years old, then you should have a certain percentage of your investments in stocks and a certain percentage in bonds. The industry has created this to assist people who are overwhelmed with their investment choices. The aim is to make it easy for the end investor to have a well-managed, diversified retirement plan.

Here's the challenge: We don't all fit into the same category as everyone else our age. Last time I checked, we were all different. I know plenty of people my age that I'm not like at all. My point is that you have to recognize where you are emotionally from a risk perspective. I have a client who, despite the fact that she's in her seventies, will forever have an aggressive growth investment style. That's how she likes it. As long as you have the risk tolerance for it, and you know your portfolio will fluctuate, then it's fine. Those who are not in touch with the level of risk they can tolerate are the ones who run into trouble. I've also found, more often than not, that people's risk tolerance changes over time.

As I've helped others amass wealth, I've noticed a fascinating pattern. People emotionally identify with dollars, not percentages. I've known clients who were perfectly fine with losing $2,000 off a $10,000 balance. On the other hand, those same people were extremely uncomfortable when they dropped $200,000 off their one-million-dollar portfolio, even though both corrections came to 20%. The total dollar amount lost was their emotional trigger. Intellectually, they clearly could see that the percentage of funds lost was exactly the same, but that was little comfort for their emotional loss. Investors have to recognize that their mindsets will change over time. The lesson here is to stay aligned with your tolerance level over the years. Keep an eye on your portfolio from an emotional standpoint or you may find that you've sold yourself—and your future—short.

Lack of Retirement Income Planning

You may think you're all set for retirement, but there are nuances to planning for your future that should not be overlooked. For example, the boomers have done a good job building up their retirement plans and other assets, but now that they're shifting to another phase of life, they need to plan for lower return assumptions and longer life expectancy. They face the risk of losing their purchasing power over time due to inflation and longevity. The fastest-growing portion of our population is 85 and older. These folks must make sure they're accounting for lack of purchasing power due to inflation. Prices are going to go up. That's just the way it is. Soon you're going to hear someone say, "I used to buy a candy bar for a dollar and now it's ten bucks!"

Who is Keeping You Off Track?

By now you should be all too aware that it isn't just *what* is holding you back, it's *who*, and some can be your nearest and dearest. What you may also not be willing to see yet is that the biggest crab in your bucket may be you!

Family, Co-Workers, Employer

I hate to say it, but family members can be big crabs. They want you to live the life *they* have envisioned for you. I can't tell you how many people I counsel who are in their fifties and still trying to please parents who are in their eighties! Do you have to wait until your parents are dead to decide that you want a different life? No way! Don't let other people's fears put limits on your desires. It's your choice whether you're going to let them do that or not.

If your employer isn't on the same page you are, *that* can also derail the fulfillment of your dreams. I recently gave a seminar at a wonderfully progressive advertising agency. I was amazed to find out how well this company had aligned its corporate goals with those of its employees by using a team approach. This company has an annual profit-sharing plan that's paid in cash—which, by the way, very few companies do today. This is really smart. Why? What do most employees want? You got it, cash! The company also takes a more holistic approach to employee performance. Each month, management hosts a "Lunch and Learn" seminar to help employees deal with personal, career, family and financial issues. A successful company is one in which everyone has a stake from top to bottom, and bottom to the top. I believe companies that add value to their employees' lives will also, in the long run, be far more profitable than their counterparts.

Lack of Personal Boundaries

We touched on boundaries in Chapter Three. Having a strong sense of self and knowing what type of treatment you will or will not accept from others makes a difference in the personal power you give away to your crabs. Do you let people get away with saying negative things to you or about you? Do you stand up for yourself in the face of conflict?

Ellen's Story

Ellen came to me twelve years ago with a debt problem. It turned out she had developed some bad habits, which harked back to her upbringing. The youngest in her family, born much later than her siblings, her parents had the resources to provide her with whatever she wanted in life. In that, she was very fortunate. As she ventured out on her own, however, she created the same pattern of giving herself whatever she wanted, whenever she wanted it. The only problem was that she was spending as if she had her parent's income, which she clearly did not. I worked with Ellen for four years to help her create a healthy financial life, one that didn't revolve around the acquisition of things. She quickly began to recognize her spending patterns and focused on becoming debt free.

To her credit, she faced the challenge head-on. Over the course of a couple of years, whenever she received a raise, we saved a portion and took another portion to pay down her debt. She also chose to use a portion of each raise to increase her lifestyle. Then, rather suddenly, Ellen stopped communicating with me. I found this very out of character. She eventually called the office to tell me what had happened. Embarrassed and ashamed, she confessed that she'd re-created the same scenario that had gotten her in trouble in the first place.

Ellen Standing In the Way of Ellen

When Ellen went incommunicado, we had been working together for about six years. Although she felt she had gotten herself into a financial mess once again, it certainly wasn't as bleak as it once was. It was manageable. Once again, she faced the challenge head-on. Ellen persevered and got herself out of debt after about another year and a half, following the same discipline of saving part of her pay raises, paying down additional debt, and allowing small lifestyle increases. Then, within a year of achieving her debt-free status, Ellen married a wonderful man who unfortunately also had a debt problem, and the whole cycle started all over again.

It soon became clear that not only did Ellen acquire some challenging spending habits from her upbringing, she also had trouble with personal boundaries. She lacked the sense of self and the necessary skills to stand up for her own money values. Consequently, she let her husband's bad habits override her own convictions. Isn't it interesting that as soon as she'd come to a place in her life where she could effectively process her financial emotions and hold money in abundance, she attracted someone who put that skill to the test? I eventually created a new assignment for Ellen. This time her challenge was to teach her hubby how to change his focus and follow the same debt—reduction exercise that she had followed and succeeded with a few years earlier. I'm a big believer that when you teach someone something, it is twice learned. This certainly was and still is the case with Ellen. I am happy to report that, with Ellen's coaching, her darling husband is on his own personal journey to financial healing, which in turn is making their marriage whole.

Self-Judgment

One of the most common obstacles I see today is the negative talk that goes on in our minds or comes out of our mouths. Believe me, the crabs that live in your head can be even more destructive than the ones on any barstool. Why? Because they disguise themselves as logic, truth and reality; they've been living in your psyche for a long time and they're all too happy to have the run of the place. I can't tell you that there's an easy way to ignore them, but I can say that learning to recognize self-defeating thoughts and words makes an enormous difference in your ability to make changes in your life. After all, our perceptions create our reality. Your mind is powerful. Why not use it to your advantage? Are you ready to take on your financial obstacles? Then don't let your head become filled with anything but positive thoughts.

Beginner's Luck

Marianne Williamson is, in my opinion, one of the most profound thought provoking, spiritual teachers of our time. Through her many books and public appearances she illuminates life's truths with brilliant and welcome insights. One of these insights particularly resonates with my soul. The gist of it is that success in life is all about beginner's luck. If you don't know the rules or haven't heard what problems are supposed to arise, you're free to be successful. In essence, whatever you expect to happen in your life is typically what does happen.

The first time I realized that I was considered "fat" was in fourth grade. Up until that time, I didn't know there was a "problem" with how I looked. Also, as far back as I can remember, I had an arch in my back that made my belly stick out. When I was a toddler, everyone thought it was cute. As I got older, that belly kept on growing, and I soon learned to tuck in my tailbone to diminish the protrusion, which is something I still do today. Well, I'll never forget this one boy in my class; let's call him Brent. He was certainly nothing to boast about; in fact, he was pudgy himself. One day we were lining up to go to gym class and he said, "Oh look, the three fattest girls in our class are all standing together!" Up until that moment, I had never viewed myself as one of the fat kids in class. That day is when my body image troubles began: in Miss Finnegan's room at Saint Christopher's School, from the lips of a ten-year-old boy.

As a side note, over the course of the year, Brent made a variety of unflattering remarks about my weight. I now believe he was really projecting his personal dissatisfaction with his own chubby physique onto me. It's amazing how often I witness this. When someone lashes out at another, it's usually because they aren't happy with the part of themselves that they see in the other person, consciously or unconsciously. For them, it's like looking in a mirror.

Your Reflections

This is sometimes difficult to swallow, but everyone who's a part of your life is a reflection of some part of you. Quite often the thing that really bugs you about someone else is a characteristic you subconsciously don't like about yourself. In a seminar I attended, we were instructed to make a list of the people that we really hate to be around. Next to their names, we were told to write down the personal traits that we didn't like about those folks. Then we had to list people we truly love to be around and their characteristics as well. The point of the exercise was that the list of good and bad traits that we'd assigned to others were actually our own. I was amazed. Those who I'm drawn to and repelled by are mirrors of me. If you could see yourself as others do, would you change your behavior? It's just a thought.

Intention at Work

When I was a freshman in high school, there was one girl I'll never forget. Let's call her Jessica. One day in study hall Jessica said to me, "You know, don't you think it's awful that it's always the popular kids who get in Homecoming Court and all that stuff?" Taking that as a challenge, I said, "Then let's be the class that changes that!" After all, why couldn't two average kids get Homecoming King and Queen? I remember Jessica laughing as she said, "Okay, Murph, we'll elect you our Homecoming Queen." I immediately started to backpedal, but then I thought, "Hey, why not?" It was almost as if a deal was struck. She vowed that in three years, when we were seniors, she'd get everyone to nominate me for Queen. At the time I remember the big eye-roll I gave her. "Yeah, sure," I said.

I was never in the popular crowd; I just tried to be nice to everyone. My mom always said, "If you don't have anything nice to say, don't say anything at all." That's still one of the best pieces of advice I ever got. Sure, I hung out with many of the popular kids because I played sports, and a lot of them did too. But I was never a member of the "in crowd." I was working all the time and I had other things to worry about. Cut to our senior year. The entire school body was convened at a pep rally in the gym for the announcement of Homecoming King and Queen. I couldn't believe it when I heard I'd been elected Homecoming Queen! And then they announced that my boyfriend was Homecoming King! Jessica walked up to me and flashed a big smile. "I told you!" she said. To say that I was in shock would be an understatement. I felt thrilled and grateful that my peers had given me this honor.

I was certainly not used to being in the limelight. I thought of myself as Cinderella, the one dressed in rags, cleaning floors, not the princess at the ball. I didn't wear the popular brand of jeans or flirt with the football guys, the usual description of a Homecoming Queen. In fact, I was the biggest crab in my bucket, and I was damn lucky my friends had more positive thoughts about me than I did about myself. This was yet more evidence that what we put our energy into becomes our reality, no matter what the circumstances.

The Queen Crab

Now for part two of the story; I was still delivering the *Chicago Tribune* and *Chicago Sun Times* every morning before school. Shortly after my victory, I saw an announcement in the paper calling all Homecoming Queens from the Midwest. There was to be a Miss Midwest Homecoming Queen selected from all the high school winners. I was secretly ecstatic. It was actually possible that I could be the Queen of all Homecoming Queens!

Later that day we were in study hall, and one of the more popular girls announced, "Hey, you guys, did you hear Julie's going to be Miss Midwest Homecoming Queen?" Her comment was met with ribald laughter. She wasn't saying this to shame or tease me; if fact, she was and still is a very nice person. But, to me, her comment pulled me down to the bottom of the bucket. I immediately joined the crowd making fun of the whole idea. Me as Miss Midwest Homecoming Queen was so laughable that I didn't even go to the pageant. To this day, I can't believe I let something I was so excited about fall right out of my lap. If only I'd faced this part of my life with that naïve beginner's luck mentality that Marianne Williamson speaks of, the ending might have been quite different. Because I didn't go, I'll never know.

16 EXERCISE

Crabs In Your Bucket Exercise

Okay, folks, you know you've got 'em. It's time to list 'em—the crabs in your bucket. If you become aware of the people who you allow to hold you back, your radar will be more likely to catch a crab in action. Think about the people around you for a minute. I want you to identify the crabs and record how they impact you. So get out that paper and pencil and let's get to it. Here are some random examples to get you started.

My boss was a big crab. He refused to give me flextime to study for my MBA and made derogatory comments about my hunger for higher education. Some days I bought into his lies and thought, "I'm never going to get this degree."

My sister is a crab. She has labeled me as "the artsy type" who will never succeed in business. I've heard this so much in my life that I sometimes believe it myself. Whenever I hit a snag at work, I hear her voice in my head saying "See, I told you so."

Now it's your turn. Put those crabs on paper. Study your list. Keep it handy, and when you encounter a new crab, write it down and intentionally choose how you'll respond. Try to shift your thinking before you encounter one of your crabs. Say to yourself: "I am a happy, healthy, intelligent person. I know what's right for me. I will not allow myself or anyone to keep me from living my ideal life." The more you say this, the more you'll believe it. Pretty soon all of your pesky crabs will sidle off into oblivion!

CHAPTER WRAP-UP

As you make changes in your life, whether emotional, physical, spiritual or intellectual, the people closest to you may pull away or reject you.

Your personal growth may cause those close to you to examine their own lives, which may make them uncomfortable. This may be a conscious or unconscious reaction.

Your friends or loved ones may try to pull you back into their world by doing or saying things that hurt you. They are just like crabs in a bucket. When one tries to escape, the others all reach up their claws to pull it back down.

Once you learn to recognize the crabs in your bucket, choose to regain your personal power and keep it for yourself. This is an important step in actualizing your ideal life.

"When you don't know who you are, you create a mind-made self as a substitute for your beautiful divine being and cling to that fearful and needy self."

—Eckhart Tolle

FACING YOUR FINANCIAL REALITY

There is nothing I value more in a person than authenticity. People who are authentic are honest with themselves in every part of their lives and aren't afraid to acknowledge their dark sides. They're more likely to be honest with their friends about their strengths and weaknesses. Self-acceptance opens the door to great personal growth and is the foundation for true intimacy on any level. It also frees us to embrace a healthier relationship with money. So let's get on with it. Out with the old and in with the new!

The next step toward financial healing is for you to be honest with yourself, to look at your life objectively—your responsibilities and realities—all of them, good and bad. Sometimes it's hard to look in the mirror. I believe this is because the minute we do, we judge ourselves. Judging accomplishes nothing. There are enough people in the world who will do that for us, so there's no need to jump on that disreputable and abusive bandwagon. When you're true to yourself and not listening to everyone else, you retain your personal power, and you're free to be the honest author of your own life, the pitch-perfect conductor of your own symphony!

A Higher Education

When I was deciding where to go to college (after having given up on Notre Dame) the only school I'd known anyone to go away to was Northern Illinois University, where my Aunt Peggy and Uncle Dave had gone. Of course I applied to what was familiar, and got accepted. At the same time, it seemed that all of my A.P. Calculus classmates at Oak Forest High School were applying elsewhere, the majority seeking admission to the University of Illinois at Urbana-Champaign. I didn't know much about the school, but I did know that if the smart kids were trying to get in there, I should too. So I sent an application there as well. The University of Illinois did not accept me for their fall semester, but, they had just begun a program called the "spring option," which allowed me to enroll for the following spring, since many students dropped out after the first semester.

I knew myself fairly well at that time in my life and was able to assess my academic abilities with objectivity. I was one of those students who came close to the top of the class but never quite crossed the threshold to the top ten. I was number twenty-three in my graduating class. I did a little research in terms of graduate income levels from U of I versus other schools like Northern Illinois. In my major, the income levels of students from U of I were higher. So were their job placement rates. This caught my eye. I felt it was worth my while to work for a semester at home, and pursue my degree from a school that would allow me a healthier salary. Had I not been able to look at my academic performance realistically, without shame or judgment, I would never have gone to the University of Illinois. If I'd let myself believe I wasn't worthy of applying because I wasn't smart enough or I just didn't belong there for some reason, I would have missed one of the most fulfilling and rewarding experiences of my adult life. As you can see, I had no self-esteem issues academically. I just wasn't real with myself when it came to matters of the flesh, namely mine!

17 EXERCISE

Life Responsibilities Exercise

I suggest that you take a few minutes right now for another quick exercise. Go back through the four aspects of the Life Navigation Wheel. This time, look at each area for what it is in the present tense. Recognize your particular responsibilities: You have kids, you have a job, you have parents, you have a spouse, you have friends. You may not like your physical body; you may not like your work. Try it; it's very empowering! Most of us were taught at a very young age to judge ourselves, to see our behavior as good or bad, right or wrong. Many forms of organized religion perpetuate self-judgment. This only stirs the pot of guilt, which has no place in building the life you want. All that's required at this juncture is objectivity. Look at your life and recognize it for what it is. Jot down your realities as fact. For example, if you know your company favors younger, cheaper labor and your quick rise to the top has ended, write it down without begrudging the point. If your spouse has a difficult time holding onto money, put that down as a statement, not a judgment. If you have all three of your children's college funds in order, that's great! Write it down. Do this with your work life, family life, personal life and financial life. But remember, no judging! Refer to your list from time to time. It's a great reminder of the facts without letting any damaging emotions get in the way.

Your Financial Dark Side

This may seem like an odd concept to you, but you should realize that your relationship with money has a dark side. We all have a shadow or dark side in some aspect of our lives. This is the side of you that flies in the face of compassion and open-mindedness and sometimes even sinks into bigotry. It's often fear-based and almost always a great distorter of truths. In the financial realm, your dark side feeds on negativity. It's the source of all unhealthy financial behavior. I recently learned a miraculous lesson about my own dark financial underbelly, and I'd like to share it with you.

I make frequent visits to Sedona, Arizona to meet with Anne Emerson, an amazing woman and gifted healer. On a recent visit, Anne gave me an assignment. I was to go off by myself and spend a couple of days recognizing the dark side of my relationship with money, then return to her with a list. I walked away thinking, "How do I do this?" The shadowy side of people is not something I tend to focus on, let alone my own. Still, I followed her instructions and returned two days later with a list of conscious and subconscious beliefs. Here is my list:

1. Money buys love.
2. Money buys freedom.
3. Money makes you happy.
4. People with excess money are not good people.
5. Money validates your character.
6. Money is the only meaning of success.

When I went back to Anne, I told her that I felt like I hadn't truly tapped into my dark side. Sure, I could list all these "lies" that I told myself from time to time, but that didn't feel restorative in the least. Anne explained to me that, as children, in an attempt to escape pain, we subconsciously bury hurtful experiences and events and the emotions they stir up. Over time, they become rooted in our minds and bodies, where they're free to flourish and grow into irrational thoughts, unhealthy behaviors and even physical maladies. She went on to say that it's painful for us as adults to pull these things to the surface. However, she explained, if I wanted to heal my dark side, I would have to confront its origin. She then lovingly guided me inward toward the early life experiences that brought me to these beliefs. I sent my mind back in time and hit the mother-lode.

There with Anne, I suddenly recalled a memory from second grade. It was in Mrs. Clark's class, the first time I ever really got in trouble at school. We were lining up for the next class period, and I was talking and laughing when we were supposed to be quiet. Busted! She immediately chastised me and gave me my first detention. For some kids, this event would come and go with little consequence, but for me it was huge. I was instantly ashamed and terrified that Mrs. Clark would no longer like me—a deep-rooted fear I had, even at age seven. I always regarded her as one of my favorite teachers, and her opinion of me truly mattered.

What happened next is fascinating to me. Instead of sitting with that fear and shame, I took action. Since it was the holiday season, I decided to buy Mrs. Clark the biggest Christmas present I could afford in an effort to win back her approval—to buy back her love. I took every dime I had earned delivering the Penny Saver and bought her a gift as an attempt to "fix" the relationship. I can't tell you how huge this insight was for me. I now realize that this was the moment of conception of an ongoing pattern of mine: Give to others to avoid or prevent rejection. This also spawned an unhealthy expectation that I have. If I buy something for you, I expect love in return. Wow, talk about setting yourself up for disappointment! I'd been trying to "buy" love for years.

Grab Bag Excess

Thanks to Anne and this memory exercise, I gained insight into my generosity with gifts, or as some would say, my *excessive* generosity with gifts. Case in point: Every year we have a family Christmas grab bag. Until recently, guess who always gave the biggest, most outrageously expensive present? That's right, *moi*. One year, after presenting one of my sisters with earrings from Tiffany's, one of my brothers pulled me aside and said that I was upsetting everyone with my thoughtless disregard for the spending limit. I thought it was just because I was a very giving person. Now I see things differently. I certainly think my generous spirit is a part of it, but in reality there's another component—my dark side. I've been seeking love and approval my entire life by using money as the means to that end, a behavior that was reinforced time and time again by unwitting participants, beginning with Mrs. Clark. This is something I'd been carrying around inside me for a very long time.

Moving Forward Through Healing

So, wow, it was great that I recognized this, but I soon found myself asking, "Now what?" I had to find a way to heal this behavior or, I knew, it would haunt me forever. I've always believed that once something emerges from your subconscious, you can never put it back. I began to spend quiet time thinking of other scenarios in my life where this same pattern played out. I discovered it was everywhere—at work, with my parents, friends, employees and other business relationships. I knew that I couldn't teach other people about money unless I challenged my own financial dark side to a one-on-one. So I made a commitment to myself that regardless of what emotions emerged, especially my fears of rejection and not being loved, I'd choose to sit with those feelings, rather than numb them by spending money, eating junk food or drinking wine. I resolved to patiently sit there with those emotions and each time they emerged, to let them pass through my psyche and my body until they dissipated and I could move past them. At first it took those buggers days to subside, and during those periods I was an emotional wreck. But over time, the dark feelings began to pass much more quickly, sometimes within seconds. Don't get me wrong, I still have urges to act out when I fear rejection or catch myself trying to force someone to love me. For the most part, I've learned to overcome the urges. I'm pretty confident that I've now banished my dark side, at least my unhealthy shadow relationship with money. Now it's your turn.

14 EXERCISE

Financial Dark Side Exercise

I invite you to explore the dark side of your relationship with money. Think about the ways you use money. Do you spend it to soothe inner pain? Do you believe that money can buy you happiness? Do you have negative feelings about people who have money, or on the flipside, people who don't have a lot of money? What internal feelings, fears, joys or emotional agitations are hiding behind your financial personality? It's okay, don't feel embarrassed. Just write them down. Unless you look at how the dark or shadow side of money is manifesting in your life, you'll never master your financial behavior and achieve financial freedom. Having your financial dark side cracked wide open can make you feel vulnerable and, possibly, a little ashamed of yourself, but it's also extremely empowering. So get over it.

The Fault Is Not in Our Stars

I'm sure it will come as no surprise to you that the most common unhealthy financial behavior is debt accrual. If that applies to you, ask yourself, "What void am I trying to fill?" If you have to, go back and reread Chapter Three to remind yourself of the influencing forces behind your financial emotions, which could be your parents, siblings, community, etc. Think about the employers you've had over the years, or the employees you've hired. Is there a personality type you're drawn to? Is that personality type a hindrance to your personal growth or happiness? Do you find yourself blaming others for standing in the way of your financial success? That used to be a big one for me. I blamed my family for "taking" my money even though *I* was the one giving it to them. Let me tell you, my friend, you're responsible for 50% of all of your relationships. If you're upset because your boss or your colleague or your spouse is taking advantage of you, it isn't their fault. It's yours, because you're the one with the "Use Me" sign on your forehead.

Carol's Story

Carol ran her own business, and when we first met she was having employee issues. It seems she continually attracted employees who came with a distrustful attitude. Every single person she hired demanded all their bonus and commission monies to be paid up front, before they were even earned. I suggested that she take a look at two things: one, how she was compensating her people, and, two, if there was a pattern of distrust in her relationships outside of work. It turned out that Carol had some issues with feeling victimized, emotionally and physically, which stemmed from childhood. This resulted in her tendency as an adult to not only control others but also to distrust them. It came as no surprise to me that she was surrounding herself with people who made demands on her, and who felt that if they didn't *take* from her, they would never *receive*.

Once Carol recognized her own behavior pattern of re-creating her childhood, she could process those victimized feelings differently. This in turn enabled her to make some healthy changes within her company. Together we created a new compensation structure that allowed her employees to keep their current salaries *and* receive bonuses based on the company's profits. This way, if the business did well, everyone did well. As time went by, during performance reviews, she gave each employee a cost of living bump, at the very least, along with a bonus percentage increase. This reinforced the notion that everyone was pulling the same wagon. Interestingly enough, over time, all but one of her original employees left. This allowed her to hire people who were better suited to her team-oriented structure. Happily, that new team of people created a phenomenal increase in sales. Just recently one of those new hires went home with a $6,000 monthly bonus check, which was double his regular paycheck. It's quite possible that every employee in her company will soon be making more in bonuses than what they earn from their already competitive salaries. Talk about putting things in alignment! And it all stems from Carol's courage to choose to emotionally heal.

Financial Karma

Before I began my spiritual journey into Eastern philosophy, I saw "karma" as some cosmic force of justice—that what goes around comes around, and that there was some higher power punishing those who wronged others. Now I view it differently, and I find that my new understanding of karma has a place in the financial realm. Simply stated, the Hindu concept of karma is that every day we make choices that create consequences. As a result, each day we face the consequences of our past decisions, every single one of them, good and bad. We are the sum of those decisions. For example, if you have a lot of debt or a lack of savings, it's typically because you made a choice to spend more than your income, or you didn't pay yourself first by putting some money into savings. Making up for past choices that create a negative present is seldom fun. Still, it provides an opportunity for personal development. Let's take this a step further. The choices that you've made in the past don't define your future; your future is defined by what you do today, what you do right now. Here is an example of what I mean. My body used to be overweight because of the food choices I'd made. Then I chose to only eat foods that fueled my body, and that became my new reality, even while my body was still overweight. Those behaviors in the present moment created a different reality in my future, which is the body that I have today.

Living In the Present Moment

The lesson here is that living in the present moment is the healthiest mindset for you if you want to make a change in your life. What's done is done. Don't beat yourself up over past choices, no matter how hard they bite you in the rear. The decisions you made in the past are just that—past, over and done with. You can't change them. You can only change the present moment, so, for goodness sake, enjoy the present moment and make the best of it. You have control over your choices today. You also have the power to influence the future, although you cannot control it. If you choose to live with positive intentions for what you want tomorrow, and you position yourself to be lucky, you stand a much better chance of getting what you want than if you did nothing at all. Live in the present. There's no other time like it.

You're close to the point of creating a shift in your life financially. Soon you'll be operating within your own framework. You'll be making the rules and following them to achieve your financial wellness. By recognizing and accepting who you are and the life that you've chosen to live, you're expressing self-love and forgiveness. This is a rewarding mindset for any aspect of life. So let's get to it!

CHAPTER WRAP-UP

People who live abundantly have chosen to see themselves objectively.

It's important to understand and acknowledge your responsibilities in life without judgment. They are the outcome of decisions you've made in the past. You cannot change the past. You can only change your behavior in the present moment, which will create your new future.

The financial choices you make in your life today create your new reality for tomorrow. I call this Financial Karma.

Learn to live in the present moment with positive intentions for your money and you'll set yourself up for success.

SECTION THREE
Financial Transformation

"When you set an intention, when you commit, the entire universe conspires to make it happen."

—Sandy Forster

SETTING YOUR INTENTIONS

Let's review where you are. You've allowed yourself to dream, you've identified some obstacles, and you accept your present status in life. You have a picture of where you wish to go. It's time to connect where you are with where you want to go in order to link your present life to what you truly desire. It's time to start mapping out your desired future!

Bite-Size Pieces

At this stage of the process, many of my clients feel overwhelmed. Getting from point A to point Z is pretty daunting if you don't know how to navigate the letters in between. I know that feeling. It's like you're on a huge cargo ship and you want to change course in a hurry, which we all know is next to impossible. If you've ever watched a freighter at sea, you know that those babies don't turn on a dime. It takes quite a bit of planning and navigational prowess for the captain to progress along a given route, let alone alter his course. After years as a financial professional, I realize that the process of shifting your focus away from surviving toward thriving is difficult. It can take up to a year and a half to two years to complete the cycle. This is perfectly fine. It's actually quite normal. Just like the captain of a ship, you must chart your path and take the journey one leg at a time.

Think of it this way: Scientists now posit that, on the quantum level, over the course of one year, 98% of every atom in your body is replaced, but not at the same time. Water molecules stay about two weeks, the atoms in your bones a few months, but not a single atom stays with you from the birth to the death of your body. Unfortunately, these new atoms don't bring back that tooth you had to have pulled last year because the new atoms learn from the old ones. But the miracle of your body is that it does do amazing things to heal itself. It takes about the same amount of time to "rebirth" your financial life—a year, more or less. You can't heal your money emotions or transform your financial status overnight. It took you time to create the reality you have today, and it will take time to create a new reality. The only way to progress is by taking baby steps. As you move forward on your journey, keep these steps in mind.

1. Brainstorm with yourself:
   a. Choose to be open to your desires and dreams.
   b. Think and write down where you want to go in every aspect of life: financial, personal, family and work.
   c. Examine where you are currently in each of those aspects.

2. Turn off that edit button:
   a. Don't judge yourself or your current reality for perceived flaws.
   b. Be objective; just acknowledge where you are at the moment.

3. Keep it simple:
   a. Start by changing one thing at a time that can get you from where you are today to where you really want to be.
   b. You may have fifty things you need to do; just pick a few to do this month.
   c. Next month, mark off a few more. Soon these little completed pieces will get you to where you want your life to be.

Internal and External Changes

Financial healing takes place in two ways: externally and internally. Just like anyone dedicated to losing weight, quitting smoking or making any lifestyle change, you must modify your day-to-day behavior, in addition to healing the inner cause of that behavior. Most psychologists will tell you that tackling both the external actions and the internal causes are the only true way to create permanent changes in any type of human behavior. Healing on the outside and the inside is the basic premise behind today's popular addiction reform programs. I won't pretend to understand drug addiction or alcoholism. The point I want to make is that I believe by connecting mind and body, we're able to transform harmful behavior into healthy actions.

Your Outer Changes

Let's talk about your day-to-day money life. In order to get from your current reality to the life you desire, a few things will have to change. When most people think about changing behavior, the daunting specter of sacrifice comes up. We all seem to believe that you have to forego certain pleasures to make gains. To me, this is simply a matter of perspective. If I choose not to spend my usual $50 a week on lunches, I don't think of myself as deprived. I look at it as making room for my new financial intentions. By not eating out every day, I'm creating a space for something new, something I desire more than lunch in a restaurant. After four weeks of this new behavior, I've saved $200 toward my goals and I still eat. I just bring myself a tasty, healthy lunch every few days.

Out With the Old, In With the New

One January afternoon in 2006, after dodging a minor avalanche of suits, skirts, shirts and random unused wedding gifts, I resolved to clean out my closets. I'd been losing so much weight that I really needed some new clothes, but there wasn't space to be found anywhere for even a single wire hanger. So I got a piece of paper and wrote down that, over the course of the year, I would get rid of twelve bags of clothing from my overstuffed closets and give them to charity. Every month, I filled a giant sack and took it to the Salvation Army. It was exciting for me to see that physical space open up. It started to feel so good that by the year's end, I'd given away thirty-six bags of perfectly good clothes I wasn't wearing.

I'm probably making this sound easier than it actually was. Some of those things were difficult for me to give away. One month, I counted sixty-two T-shirts that needed to go into the bag. Why was this difficult? Well, they all had sentimental value. I had a shirt from just about every destination I had visited in my twenties. Luckily, one of my cousins had an idea. We cut out the logos from every shirt and she made them into a quilt. Very few things make me cry, but I'll tell you when she showed me the finished piece, it was as if all the memories wrapped up in those shirts came to life. It's an awesome quilt and I love using it. Even better, I'm now down to a mere fifteen T-shirts. What's equally remarkable is that I resolved to give those shirts away and they came back to me in a more useful form.

Your money works the same way. If you want something other than what you have today, you need to make space for it. Even if your intention is funding a savings account with $5.00 per paycheck, you can find ways to make room for it. Having one less latte during the week makes space for that savings account to grow. Make space, make space, make space! This will allow the flow of money to start.

19 EXERCISE

Make Room for Abundance Exercise

Take a moment to think about what you could remove from your current life to make room for your new life. Go back and revisit the Life Navigation Wheel that you created in Chapter Five. Looking at your ideal life, make a list of what you could do to make room for those things to occur. Another way to look at it is to ask, "What doesn't support my dreams?" It could be anything from the food in your fridge to the clothes in your closet, from your job, to your house, to your personal prejudices. It could be the magazines you have lying around that tempt you to buy unnecessary stuff. It could be pictures of old friends or your ex-boyfriend or girlfriend. Maybe she's hanging around too. You have to physically move out the old to make room for the new! Don't limit it to material things—it could also be people. Which friends are really not supporting you in your desire to change and move forward? Write down everything you can think of. No one else will see your list, so don't hold back. When you're done, choose at least one thing that you recorded and commit to removing it from your life. Trust me, you'll find it most rewarding.

Get in the Flow—the Cash Flow

Whether or not you've ever worked with a financial professional or wealth advisor, you probably have money flowing toward different areas of your life. This may surprise you, but I personally don't like the word "budget." Let me rephrase that. I hate that "b" word. It feels confining and, to be honest, carries a lot of baggage. I prefer to think of this relationship with your money as "directing your flow." We all have cash flow, money coming in and going out. For some, that flow resembles a graceful river. For others, it looks more like white-water rapids. In either case, you most likely have a paycheck from your employer or your own company that brings in income, and that money is then allocated to different destinations, such as your checking account, maybe a savings account, retirement fund, etc. Let's set that aside for a moment.

Energy, the New Currency

For the next few minutes I want you to forget everything you've ever learned about cash flow. I don't even want you to think about money as dollar bills, coins, checks, credit cards or account balances. Instead, I want you to think of money as a form of energy. It's an energy that flows through your life. It can be positive energy or it can be negative energy.

Now that you're in this frame of mind, consider these questions:

- ✓ Where do you focus your energy?
- ✓ Do you dwell on how little you have or how to acquire more?
- ✓ How do you nourish this energy?
- ✓ What do you think you're doing that slows or blocks the flow?
- ✓ What or who around you drains you of that energy?
- ✓ Do you store that energy for a later date or do you burn it continuously?

Now I'd like you to bring money back into the picture. Merge your notion of money with the energy metaphor we just created. Picture yourself writing a big check to pay towards a big credit card bill. I bet you feel the energy draining right out of your toes, don't you?

I asked you to follow that exercise to demonstrate that money isn't just about cash. It's about energy too. The cash itself isn't all that powerful or daunting by itself. But add energy to the mix, and it's explosive. How you choose to let both your money and energy flow will make all the difference in your life.

Money and Energy Are One

Here's another way to look at money and energy. The action of borrowing money involves the flow of two distinct streams. One is the literal stream of money between the lender and the borrower. The other is the stream of energy flowing between the two. Although they are separate elements, together they create one financial dynamic. Just as you can't remove hydrogen or oxygen from water and still have water, you can't separate the energy from the money and still have a financial transaction. If a lender gives you $10,000 and you pay it back with 7% interest, that's a positive money flow, and a positive energy flow. It's a fair and balanced relationship and the door is still open for you to collaborate in the future.

What if, however, one of the parties doesn't hold up their end of the bargain? Say (heaven forbid!) you fail to pay back the money according to your agreement. The flow of money between you and your lender becomes disrupted. This also corrupts the flow of energy within the transaction. The borrower/lender relationship is severed and you must go elsewhere to find another source for money. What's more, you've no doubt created a bad mark on your credit report. You're now swimming against the surging tide of negative energy and negative cash flow. This is not just exhausting; it creates the potential for financial calamity.

Directing Your Flow

So what about that cash flow? Does yours serve a purpose or is it a rambling stream, wandering here and there? Remember, how much you make isn't as important as what you do with it once it comes in. Your intentions for your money are the difference between surviving and thriving. If you're an extreme planner, you might direct a huge chunk of cash toward your retirement. If you're a spender, perhaps every dime of your income goes toward eating out, entertaining friends or buying lavish gifts for yourself and for others. Most folks are somewhere in the middle of those two extremes. Regardless, if you have cash coming in the door, you must ask yourself what your personal strategy is. What do you want that money to do for you? Successful wealth-building relies on setting intentions for your income in three different segments, or buckets: Short-term, Mid-term and Long-term. We're going to dip into those buckets in a minute, but first I want to impress upon you the importance of your intent.

Intention in Motion

The intentions you set with your money are extremely powerful. As I mentioned in Chapter Four, creating an intention is a spiritual process that links our desires to the physical world. It's a miraculous and momentous event, one we all have the freedom and the ability to partake of. Isn't it remarkable that something so life-changing can be so easy? All you have to do is want something, and then live like it's already yours.

You have an intention power source within you. If you have completed the exercises in this book up to now, you're ready to tap into it, and set your intentions for your ideal life. These intentions will help drive you, in the days, weeks and months ahead, close to your goals. They will aid you in making wise choices on the day-to-day level by keeping you focused on the bigger picture.

20 | EXERCISE

Money Intention Exercise

In order to make your intentions real, you need to refer to your Life Navigation Wheel once more. If you choose to live the life you've envisioned, you must set financial intentions to get there. We're going to start where you're comfortable. It doesn't matter if it's big or small; just be where you are now, emotionally. Using Lego blocks, imagine that you want to create a four foot replica of the Statue of Liberty. You have to start with just one humble little block. What we're doing here is no different. You're going to spread your dreams out on the floor and look at them. Then choose one to begin sculpting your new life.

Now, take a look at the dreams you listed next to each circle on your wheel. I'd like you to focus on just one. It could be from any of the four areas: Work, Family, Personal or Financial. Do you have it? Good. On a piece of paper, make a list of what you could do financially to achieve your goal. It could be all kinds of things, from changing how you spend, to saving a certain amount of cash each month. It could be researching a new career or breaking up with your boyfriend or girlfriend. Don't hold back. What feels right to you? What resonates with you? Do you have any goals in your life that you'd like to fulfill? Is there anything that feels like you're at war with yourself? A fight between your heart and your mind? When you feel you're ready, read back over your list. Select one or two actions that excite you the most. Don't think about how big or small they seem, or how easy or difficult they will be for you to master. Just write them down on a single piece of paper like this:

In order to reach my dream of _____, I will _____.
Or you could write:
I choose to _____ in order to manifest my life's desire of
_____.

As you fill in the blanks, project yourself to the day you're actually living the life you created. Feel the excitement, the joy and the gratitude, as if it has already occurred. In addition to writing your intentions, I invite you to make signs or cut out pictures that depict your new life. Put them where you can see them daily. Make a collage you can hang up. Honor them, revere them. These intentions are your golden ticket to nirvana. Treat them like the precious gems they are.

Identifying Intentions for the Authentic You

There are some questions you can ask of yourself to connect with your authentic self. What are you drawn to? What is true for you first and foremost? What is your heart's desire? Look at these questions from three timelines: short-term, mid-term and long-term. It's not just about tapping into your ideals for the here and now; what's really true for you will be consistent. We've already established that how we use money is a form of energy, so we need to make sure our intentions are consistent with how we want this energetic flow of money to be. It's the consistency that's the tricky part for most people.

Your inner voice, that self-talk that forms your spirit, can either free you or hold you down. Which do you choose? Think of at least one positive statement about what you want your money to do for you. You can think of it as a statement, a mantra or anything else—that doesn't matter. Its purpose is to assist you in manifesting your ideal world. It could be something like, "Money will abundantly flow to me with immediacy and ease." It doesn't have to be just one statement either; it can be many, to add to or change as time goes on.

Setting Intentions for My Business

One year I decided to set intentions for my business. It was going to do $60,000 plus per month for that calendar year. When I first formed this intention, I was getting referrals that were high quality, and current clients of mine were getting huge raises and inheritances. Notice I didn't put a limit on myself, saying $60,000 only; I said "$60,000 plus." You must be very precise in what you're asking for, from the timeframe down to the exact specifics, because this is what you'll create. Interestingly, my physical body started to get a bit weird and I had an uncomfortable feeling in my stomach. For a couple of months, the revenue started to slow down and I realized I was doing things that were blocking the flow of income. I had let go of my intention. So I made sure that every day I got back to saying, "My accounts receivable and revenue will be $60,000 plus every month." It started to flow. It was almost as if I'd turned on a faucet. I decided to test my intention method further. I said to myself, "My accounts receivable and revenue will be $100,000 plus every month." It took a few months to align properly, but the income started to flow into my business at an even greater rate. Again it spooked me, and again it slowed me down, but I renewed my intention once more, and it kept on working.

Oddly enough, sometimes it's difficult to stay open and allow yourself to receive abundance, particularly when it's exactly what you want. I don't know about you, but I was not raised that way. One of my teachers and now a friend Karyn Pettigrew, who's an inspired "business healer," told me that once you begin to manifest these things in your life, say as they occur, "Thank you! More please!" After these blockages happened, you better believe I kept saying, "Thank you, more please!" every day. My focus has been to create and manifest more and more of my life's purpose. I define that as being "To live an abundant life and to teach others to discover and live an abundant life." Give it a try. I know, it may sound goofy, and you better bet your shorts that my dominant left brain was pulling out all the stops and questioning how logical this really is. There was just a part of me that was curious enough to put it to work, so I did. Now, I can't turn it off. Quite frankly, I don't want to. Why would I?

For those of you who are parents, and your adult "logical" mind starts getting in the way, share this concept with your kids. They are amazing sponges when it comes to learning and especially harnessing something new. My nephew, Matuka, and niece, Brittany, floor me all the time. You don't really realize how much they absorb from you. I encourage them to think about what they really, really want and repeat it to themselves, saying that it will become reality. One day my sister, Marianne, gave me a call and said, "Julie, you're never going to believe this one." I have to preface this story with some more details about my nephew. He's on the honor roll and rarely misses a day of school. But one day, Matuka was feeling really tired and went to bed early, feeling like he needed a break. The next morning he got up for school and he said, "Mom, I really don't want to go to school today. Can I stay home?" Marianne works full time, so it is not an easy decision to have her kids stay home. But this particular day, the doctor she worked for was out of town. Marianne told me that since Matuka had been doing such a great job in school, she told him he could stay home. Her son jumped out of bed and started to celebrate, "Yes, yes, yes!" My sister looked at her son and said, "I thought you weren't feeling good." He said, "Mom, last night before I went to bed and this morning I kept saying to myself, I want mom to let me stay home, and it happened!" Things came into alignment, even down to my sister's job allowing this event to occur. Strange, but true, every word! I'm certainly not encouraging children to stay away from school, but this was the result of intention. Matuka had worked hard and was on the honor roll; his mom had the day off work; and he needed to take a break, just as adults sometimes do.

Be Careful What You Wish For...?

There's a caveat to this law of attraction. I have a family member who was always saying her spouse was this or that, with a lot of blame to her spin. They were on their way down the unhealthy path to a potential divorce. Well, guess what, she was helping to create more of the things she didn't want, because this was exactly what she was energizing. We had a long conversation about her marriage, and I said, "Why don't you try to find the things you really appreciate in your relationship with your husband? Reward the behavior you want, instead of complaining about the stuff you don't want." She started to recognize that the more she complained to him about how crappy he behaved the crappier their relationship became. So one day she tested it out. She thanked him for scraping his plate after dinner, instead of complaining that he didn't wash the dish.

It was as if she shifted the entire energetic connection between the two of them. The next day, she found more to thank him for. Then he started to kiss her goodnight, which he hadn't done in a long time. One day, it was snowing outside, and as they were going about their morning ritual as usual, her husband came back into the house. She thought he'd left for the day, but he said, "I just wanted to tell you I started your car and I brushed all the snow off it." She was thrilled. She rewarded more of the behavior she wanted, showed some gratitude, and said thank you! This was five years ago, and today they are much happier. I had to laugh one day when I heard her giving the same advice to another family member, recounting how doing so had changed the dynamics of her and her husband's entire relationship. You have to realize that in life, your participation is 50% of what goes on in your world. Until you admit that, you will keep spinning your wheels.

Interestingly, while doing research on my book, I came across a definition of the word "millionaire" as happiness and abundance. Who wouldn't want happiness and abundance? So come on, let's become millionaires. Make your life deliberate; set up your life with your own intentions, not anyone else's. Don't give away that personal power. Your inner touchstone, your positive inner voice, your intuition can guide you better than anything else out there in the external world. If you feel like you're tied down in life, say to yourself every day, "I am free" and you will begin to be free.

Perhaps the most difficult part is to refrain from questioning these statements of intention and desire. The minute you start to give in to those crabs of doubt, they pull you down and become your reality. Remember when I couldn't believe that $60,000 per month was coming into the business? You have to believe you deserve your ideal life. Everyone knows the Biblical saying, "You reap what you sow." What are you doing that's clipping your own wings and preventing you from soaring in your life? What are you attracting? If your self-talk is not positive, change it! Also, it's important to be persistent. Things may not shift immediately. There is no instant gratification here, which I know is tough for many of us in the Western world to accept, but be patient. It's like working out at the gym. You need to build up your muscles, day by day. It takes time.

Bucket Intentions

Now we're ready to talk about those buckets. In order to fund them with your intentions, you have to know how they're set up to work for you (see Figure 6). This will require dipping your toes into the deep end of financial jargon for a brief paragraph or two.

Figure 6

Short - Term
(1 year money)

Saving Accounts
(3-6 months in
emergency reserves)
Online Savings Accounts
Certificates of Deposit
(CDs)
Money Market

Mid - Term
(3-10 year money)

Stocks
Bonds
Mutual Funds
Real Estate Investment
Limited Partnerships

Long - Term
(10+ year money)

Employer Retirement Plan
Roth IRA
Cash Value Life Insurance
Annuities
After-Tax IRA

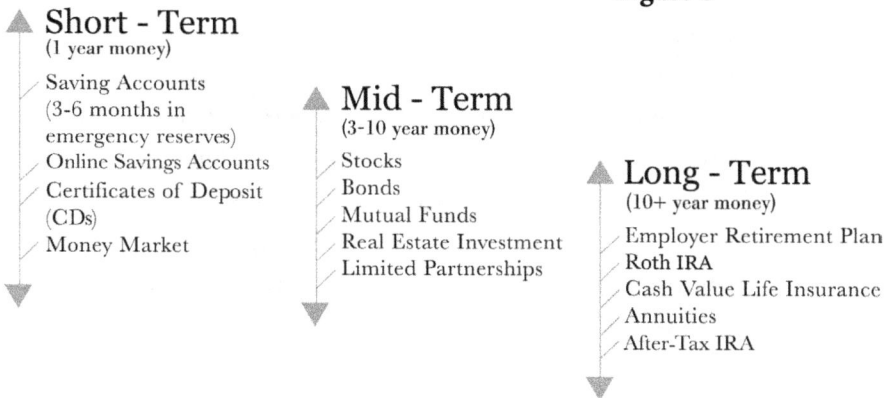

Short-Term Bucket

This is where it's good to have three to six months of living expenses set aside. How much exactly depends on your emotional comfort level. By nature, I'm a bit of a risk taker. For some people, if it were up to them, they'd have enough to live on for an entire year in this kind of account, while I'm okay with cutting it pretty close at only one month of emergency reserves. Sometimes when operating as a couple, people have had to come up with a compromise so that both comfort levels are addressed. If you're married or in a relationship, it's important that you take into account both opinions and find a harmonic solution.

The types of accounts for short-term expenses are savings and checking accounts, money markets, and CDs, along with a new vehicle called "electronic savings accounts," which you can manage by yourself online. There's really nothing complicated about any of these accounts. They are the most basic savings products, and since safety is the foremost consideration, they don't offer a huge rate of return. Their chief advantages are that they are liquid, and usually insured by the Federal Government (FDIC). Personally, I prefer electronic savings accounts for short-term savings. Because it's an online bank of sorts, there's far less overhead, which means a slightly higher rate of return for you. Plus you get instant access to your account via the Internet, and your money is FDIC insured.

Mid-Term Bucket

Your mid-term bucket holds what I like to call "three-to-five-year money." Most people don't have a mid-term bucket. They are either too heavy in short-term or too heavy in long-term. It's funny, most older people tend to overfill their short-term buckets and younger people typically heavy-up their long-term savings. Of course, this is all based on emotions. Mid-term accounts have higher risk, but typically higher returns than short-term ones. Mutual funds, stocks, bonds, real estate investment trusts, real estate or mortgage limited partnerships—these are all examples of mid-term monies.

I find that this is a great place to have real estate investments, since the IRS rules on real estate can be advantageous. What's more, because the property market fluctuates less dramatically than the stock market, you avoid the emotional and financial roller-coaster of NASDAQ and the like. If you've never seen yourself as the landlord type, don't worry. Today there are ways to hold real estate without having to manage the property yourself. These are called real estate investment trusts (REITs); there are also real estate limited partnerships which I mentioned earlier. If it fits with your emotional makeup, consider putting some of your mid-term assets into property investments. I'm not talking about the house that you live in. That doesn't count as a real estate investment, because you're not going to sell it without buying or renting another place to live. Your house should never be considered a source of cash flow unless you have a multi-unit property.

College planning also falls into the mid-term category. The now popular 529 Plan, which allows you to contribute up to $250,000, tax-deferred, can be used for higher education. The gains are not taxed at all when used for higher education. Again, this is just an option. If it makes sense to you intellectually and emotionally, by all means consider putting money into a 529 Plan. When I first got into the industry, cash value life insurance policies were frequently used for tax-deferred cash accumulation for education. Since then, the IRS has come out with a few other great college planning accounts like the 529 to help your money go farther. An interesting pattern is emerging in the realm of government tax assistance. Many of the newer tax laws now encourage us to take care of our own financial future. What a novel idea!

Long-Term Bucket

You're probably pretty tuned into this bucket because it contains money earned in a 401(k), 403(b) or 457 Plan. Don't let the alphabet soup confuse you. These are all just different types of retirement products. Regardless of which IRS code is used to describe it, this is your retirement money. I tell all my clients with these types of plans to max out the "free money" from their employer. What this means is that if your employer has a matching program, take full advantage of it. Another retirement option is a Roth IRA, which allows you to save up to $5,000 a year, depending on your income. The difference between a Roth IRA and accounts like a 401(k) and a regular IRA is that the gains on a Roth IRA can be tax-free when you take your money out after age 591/2, whereas the interest earned on a 401(k) is taxable when you take distributions, even after age 591/2. The Roth was initiated as part of the Taxpayer Relief Act of 1997. The government, in my opinion, introduced this and other retirement savings plans because the Social Security system is not in a healthy state. It's Washington's remedy for a failing infrastructure, and we should all be grateful for the alternative.

There are other options such as annuities, available for retirement savings. I find that there are various opinions and a lot of confusion about annuities. Without getting too technical, there are three different types of tax-deferred annuities: fixed, equity-indexed and variable. A variable annuity is like a 401(k) plan in that you have a portfolio of investments to choose from. Fixed annuities are like the CDs you open at a bank, but the fixed rate is usually higher than most CDs. Equity-indexed annuities come with a guarantee of principal, but they are measured against something that happens in the stock market. This is what makes them an index investment. The annuity that is right for you depends on your emotional need to have guarantees. There are higher expenses inside annuity contracts, and this makes them less popular for some financial professionals. Still, it's never wrong to buy something if it makes you feel better. Remember, you need to satisfy both your financial and emotional needs, and don't let anyone tell you otherwise.

What's In Your Bucket?

I'd like for you to think of these buckets as tools. Just as you use a hammer or wrench for building or repairs, you can use your buckets as instruments to help you build or repair your financial reality. Take a minute and think about your current cash flow as it relates to these three buckets. Again, don't judge yourself. Just take a minute to raise your own awareness of where your money flows. Are you funding all three buckets on a monthly or quarterly basis? And, if so, how much is going into each? Are you heavier in the long-term than in the short-term? Maybe you aren't really dividing your money for any kind of savings. Maybe you're feeling like a victim of limited income, or unusually lucky that you just happen, whatever the case, to have your cash flowing in abundance, but fear someday your luck may run out. I can't reiterate enough that you are responsible for how your money flows.

What's true for you in your less-than-one-year time horizon?

What do you currently have in your short-term bucket? Is that the reality that you want, moving forward? If not, in your ideal world, what would you like as cash in the bank, as a reserve to be able to get at some cash quickly, if you had an emergency?

I find that too many people today use their credit cards as their emergency reserves. The greatest challenge here is that you lose control. In other words, you lose your ability to manifest intentions, because no credit card company is going to say, "Fine, no problem," if you tell them, "Sorry, I can't pay that bill for my past emergency because I'm setting my intentions in another direction." You have to then deal with the reality of past choices, and it's a hard cycle to shift. It can be done, but you have to do something different or you won't get a different outcome.

This is where the emotional numbers take over the financial numbers. If you're constantly only paying off debt, and that's where your focus is, that's the only financial picture you're going to keep creating. As I said before, I don't care if it's only $5.00 per month that you put in a cash reserve fund to start. It's setting the intention that will create a new reality. Eventually, with consistent follow through, you will have no debt and a nice emergency fund built up as well. You do need to have some cash saved for the proverbial rainy day. Then when and if life throws you for a loop, you have a contingency plan, and you won't have given your personal power over to a credit card company.

What's true for you in your mid-term bucket—your three-to-ten-year picture?

What intentions would you like to set for the three-to-ten-year window in your life? Do you want a new home? Are you yearning for a new car? A boat? A new job? Is your family life what you want it to be? Kids? Would you make any changes to your family life? If there's something that you're uneasy about in your current family scenario, what is it, and how can you change it? Do you want to move to a warmer climate? Retire? What's true for you about your current job? Do you want to shift careers? What does that look like? Once you know where you want to go, you can align your money to support those dreams and desires.

In my mid-thirties, I realized that one day I did want to have children. Since I spent so much time raising my siblings, I had always questioned whether it was or wasn't important to me. From a financial perspective, if I decided children would eventually become part of my life and my intention, I couldn't work 70-hour weeks any longer. I'd need to start sooner rather than later to create a team around me who would share in the revenues of my business so that I'd have people in place who cared about my company as much as I do. Then, when I needed to work 30-40 hour weeks, I'd have the confidence that not only would the business still operate, but also that my clients would be well taken care of. I'd have to find people who have the same value system as I do. My clients are my family, and I know I also need to do what's right for my life.

I set my intentions to find those pillars of strength and responsibility, people who were entrepreneurial by nature and could do what they loved to do inside my firm. One by one, they all came into my life. I had the perception that I would take a financial hit to set up this new reality; then I realized I was creating it. I decided to set my intention to have it all—a great family life, great work life, great financial life, and great personal life—and I'm happy to say that it's all coming together quite nicely. Again, we just have to realize how we each create our own reality.

What's true for you in your long-term bucket—your ten-years-plus timeframe?

I'm convinced that we were not put on this earth to burn ourselves out. Instant gratification is causing many of us to shift our personal power to money. As a result, many of us have to work more hours and more years to solidify our own future. I've never met anyone who wanted to work the rest of their lives because they had to. Certainly, I've met people, and I believe myself to be one of them, who will always do some type of work because they really, truly love what they do. But having to work is not the same as wanting to work; they are two completely different paradigms. That being said, what's true for you in your long-term horizon? Do you want to work part-time at some point in your life to take advantage of more traveling or other opportunities in your life? How do you envision what your semi-retired or retired years will be? Many people know they need to address their retirement planning, but most are just trying to deal with the here and now. The reality of it is that you must consider both, because they will both become your reality at some point.

This book is all about setting you up for an abundant financial life, but in order for it to work, you can't really separate the financial from the other aspects of your life. Everything radiates from the center, which is your authentic self. I truly believe that all you need to do is build everything in your world around that center. As counterintuitive as it may seem, money will flow when you follow your innermost desires, your dreams. Make your dreams the drivers in your life, and you will be in high integrity with your soul.

As I said earlier, your current balances are the fulfillment of your financial karma—the result of past choices you have made. The amount of money you have in any account, fund or policy never has been, and never will be, the result of some magical, mystical process. Your current balances are a fact of your past choices. They are there because of you. Now that you have a sense of what you want out of life, you can use your personal power to get you to your ideal life.

Setting Intentions with Life Phases and Flow

New clients always ask me to advise them about how much they should have in each bucket. I believe there are no generic shoulds to building wealth. If someone tells you how much you should have in each area, they aren't in tune with you and your money emotions. Shoulds imply that there is an effective one-size-fits-all approach to wealth. Not true! How you apportion your flow depends on your core values, personal goals and dreams, coupled with your phase of life—not to mention how you feel about your money. Got it? Good. Whether you currently have millions or a more humble cash base, it's important to examine your buckets in two ways:

1. What are your current balances in each bucket?

2. What amount do you contribute to each bucket monthly or otherwise?

Of course, the answer to those two questions will be intimately tied to your financial intentions. But there is another consideration, and, for the vast majority of people, it's the primary factor. I am speaking of your current phase in life. After all, those of us in our thirties are focused on needs that are different from our older peers. Here are the top considerations for each age group that I typically discuss with my clients in preparation for creating a Life Navigation Plan. By bringing these common realities into the mix, along with your personal desires, we can get a much broader view of your life.

In Your Twenties

- Do you have to start paying down student loan debt?

- Are you purchasing a new car?

- Are you purchasing a first home? (Do you want it paid off by the time you're 40? You potentially can if you have a 15-year mortgage.)

- Do you have marriage plans?

- Do you have children? What can you do about saving for college?

- Do you have a career you're passionate about?

- Are you wrestling with thoughts of success or failure?

- What are you choosing to do in your personal, financial, work and family life?

- Do you want to donate your time or money to those in need?

- Give yourself permission to have it all!

In Your Thirties

- Are you now buying a second home and selling your first home?

- What is your marital status now?

- What can you do about saving for your children's college education?

- Have you done any estate planning for guardianship of children, etc.?

- Do you need to stop that runaway credit card debt train?

- Are you letting go of the things you can't control in your life and changing the things you can?

- Are you creating the space you need for yourself?

- What kind of financial karma are you tossing around?

- Do you live a life of financial lack or financial abundance?

In Your Forties

- Are you still passionate about your work or is it time to move on?

- Are you starting over in the wake of financial loss?

- Is your risk tolerance the same now with regard to your money and what it's doing for you?

- Are you on track to financial independence? Are you on the path to enough income to work less, and if so, at what age?

- What's fresh in your life? What feeds your soul?

- What is the biggest obstacle to having the life you desire?

- What life have you chosen thus far?

In Your Fifties

- Do you have to care for aging parents?

- How do you want to define your life from this point forward?

- Do your legal documents need to be updated?

- What legacy do you want to leave behind?

- Do you want to begin to reduce your workweek to enjoy more of other aspects of life?

- What intentions will you set once you get the biggest pay raise of your life (house becoming paid off and/or kids no longer in college)?

- What aspect of your life do you want to energize with this new open cash flow?

- Do you want to start a new career?

In Your Sixties

- Do you plan to retire sooner or later?

- If you retire, do you have to take a pay cut or downsize?

- You're only at halftime, so what's your life's purpose now?

- Does your investment management strategy still match your goals now that you're shifting from accumulation to distribution years?

- Are you still caring for aging parents?

- Are you supporting your grandchildren's dreams?

- Review the questions for your 50s!

In Your Seventies

- What are you going to do to stay actively engaged in your personal, financial, work and family life? What are you doing to keep the mind and body going?

- How has your risk tolerance changed for your investments?

- Do you want to start gifting money to your heirs, if at all?

- Do you have plans for retirement, travel, hobbies, pleasure, moving to a smaller, more manageable home in a better location?

- Any regrets? Any unmet goals that you want to accomplish? (I had one client who went to law school in his 70s. Harriet Doerr published her first novel at age 73.)

- Review the questions for your 50s and 60s!

In Your Eighties

- You're in the fastest-growing age group. Now what?

- Are you staying active and engaged? (Daniel Schorr, reporter and NPR commentator, is still not retired at age 83.)

- What's really important to you in your life from this point forward?

- Review the questions for your 60s and 70s!

Credit Cards and Cash Flow

I'd like to point out that not everyone has a clear view of their current financial picture. Heavy credit card use prevents you from seeing your true cash flow. I said it before and I'm going to say it again: There's something energetically different about handing over $1,800 cash to buy a plasma screen TV and swiping a credit card for that same $1,800 purchase. There is no real sense of responsibility or accountability with credit card use. There is 100% responsibility when you spend cash. Charging your everyday expenses can turn into an unhealthy financial practice for two reasons. The first reason is because it allows you to spend beyond your means. Does this sound familiar? "If I don't have to pay it off every month, why not let the credit card company float me the funds?" This is the kind of thinking that perpetuates a cycle of survival, not prosperity. The second problem with your money flowing through credit cards is that you will most likely waste money on unnecessary fees. Even if you have every good intention in the world to pay off that balance each month, send in one late payment and there goes fifty bucks right out the door. That's your fifty dollars, not theirs! If there is only one piece of advice you take from this book, let it be this—if you can't say no to excessive spending, you should avoid using credit cards all together. Choose to operate on a cash basis!

Remember, you have to position yourself to be lucky. Guide your money toward the places and financial products that will bring you your dreams. Make a conscious choice to alter the spending habits that stand in your way. If that means canceling your line of credit, I'll wait here while you go make the phone call. Trust me, I've heard every reason under the sun why people keep credit cards, from the need for airline tickets (earned from points) to funding their fetish for expensive shoes. Don't get me wrong, all your reasons are valid; after all it's about you, remember? The trouble is that most people don't reserve their credit cards exclusively for special or sacred use. Marketing gimmicks like free merchandise or frequent flyer miles don't even begin to make up for what you're paying out in interest and late fees, not to mention the freedom you're giving up by going to work every day to pay for all of those past purchases. If you're living on credit, you've pigeonholed yourself as a debtor, and it will be extremely challenging to escape the chaos of survival!

Chris's Story

Chris is the hiring manager for the North American division of a multinational company. He and his wife had a vision of their dream home years before it became a reality. They were both raised in fairly traditional middle class homes. Chris was the first college graduate from his family, and his wife was a preschool teacher. When we met, Chris had spent 15 years of his life working hard and moving up the ranks. His wife chose to work in the home, raising their two children. When I met them, Chris and his wife had their sights set on lakefront property in the prestigious Chicago suburb of Wilmette. At the time, they knew it was out of their reach. When Chris and his wife went through the Life Navigation Wheel with me, they weren't afraid to say exactly what they wanted the home of their dreams to be like. As the couple assessed the obstacles they faced in purchasing the house—from his job security and cash flow to their two children's private school tuition—they realized that with the right adjustments, they could achieve their dream in four years. We then devised an action plan to get them there. In essence, Chris and his wife set their intentions on that house and made the necessary changes in their cash flow to get there.

The first thing we did was examine their cash outflow to determine if all of those items were as important as their dream home. They both agreed they could cut back on a few of their expenses, such as dining out and taking less extravagant vacations. Chris even chose to take the train in to work during the summer months to save on parking. We then diverted those same dollar amounts that were going out of pocket into an account called "Dream Home." It really wasn't much at first; they had initially cut only $50 per month from their expenditures. But they were intent on saving for that home. I also had them look through magazines of homes and start to map out the specifics of their dream. I told them to cut out pictures and put them up on the fridge or anywhere else that would help remind them of what was important to them. After the second year, they were socking away about $300 a month in the "Dream Home" fund.

As the savings account grew, so did their sense of urgency. I see this happen often, and it's great. Once someone witnesses their dream becoming a reality, their actions kick into high gear. When we think our dreams are out of touch, any attempt to reach them seems futile. But when we put them on a clear path, we're motivated to sprint toward the finish line. Chris and his wife soon found other places to save. They chose to say no to high-ticket purchases; they cut back on their vacation spending by making smaller trips as opposed to large ones that drained their cash. They put everything they would have spent into their "Dream Home" savings account. They were about a year away from manifesting their dream home when Chris got an extra boost. Some would chalk it up to coincidence; I believe it was the power of the couple's intent. His employer announced they were going to give a larger than normal bonus that year. The dollar amount just happened to be the last chunk of money they needed to seal the deal. Needless to say, their new mortgage was more than the last one, but the money we carved out on a monthly basis to save for the house was enough to cover the new mortgage.

This story is a perfect example of how easy it is to redirect your cash flow. Just set your intentions for what you want your cash to do. It's that easy.

Finding the Money to Fund Your Flow

Now, what if you're stretched to the max every month, without extra cash to put into all three buckets? What if your financial inbox and outbox are one and the same? There are a few ways to "find" extra money:

1. Stop getting a big tax return. That's right. Change your withholdings on your W-4 so your paycheck is bigger and your refund goes away. You want to break as close to even as you can in April. Why let the Feds earn a penny of interest on your money—money that you could be investing in your own buckets and earning interest on? Calculating your withholdings is more of an art than a science, but here is a

rule of thumb to follow: For every $1,500 you get back, increase your exemptions by one. That little worksheet on the W-4 form you fill out at the office does not take into account deductions like mortgage interest, children or education credits. Before you tell me that you really like getting that lump sum back, consider this: Wouldn't you rather create your own interest-bearing lump sum to which you have complete access?

2. Save that raise, or at least part of it. Whenever your employer ups your paycheck, no matter how meager the raise, take at least half that extra amount and use it to fund one of your buckets. This is newfound money. Why not put it toward some part of the future that you want to create? Think of it this way: Even if you only get a 2% raise, if you save half of it for five years in a row, you've just increased your savings level by 5%.

3. If you can, escrow your real estate taxes yourself. Many lenders only require that you pay into their account for one year. Check with your mortgage company to see if you can set aside the money for your taxes. That way you'll be earning the interest, not them!

Setting Your Intention to Make Inner Changes

So what about all of those feelings, drives and urges deep down that cause you to handle money as you do? For some people, they are right on the surface and easy to recognize. Others must do a little psychological excavation to get at them. Still, they are worth digging for. There are a lot of great self-help books out there to help you get in touch with your emotions. There are also plenty of talented therapists, social workers and counselors who are trained to bring those emotions to light and help you heal any inner wounds. What's important though is that you see yourself as unique and special. There's nothing wrong with you, but there are better ways to respond to inner conflict.

In Search of Murph Man

Throughout my college years and beyond, every guy I dated was the same as the next. There was a definite pattern—about 5'10", somewhat athletic but not a total jock, attractive but not a pretty boy, a healthy and stocky frame. Each one walked and talked the same, and even treated me in a similar male—dominating fashion. My close friends dubbed any man who fit this profile as a "Murph Man." They thought it was hilarious. I began to find it quite curious that my suitors were all so similar. I also found it interesting that I never let my relationship with any "Murph Man" get too serious

My Marriage Intention Changes

Inside, I felt at odds with myself. I was a smart, independent young woman, eager to step into the fast lane of finance, yet my traditional Catholic upbringing (the tribal pull of the first chakra) kept me looking for a man who expected me to be a traditional wife. There was a constant tug-of-war going on inside my mind and body. Then I met Dillon. Dillon was a perfect "Murph Man" on the outside, but on the inside he was different. He was far less chauvinistic than the others. He was softer, more open-minded and more accepting of a career-oriented female. Still, he enjoyed kids and looked forward to having a wife and family of his own someday. Without even trying, over the course of our six-month relationship, Dillon awakened something in me. He helped me see that there was room for both Julies in my life—the career-oriented woman and the nurturing mom and wife. Although we didn't stay together, Dillon gave me a tremendous gift, the opportunity to learn something about myself and the choice to change a pattern of behavior that had imprisoned me for decades.

Don't Change for Change's Sake

It's true that I could have changed my pattern of behavior when it came to dating men without looking inward as to why I chose those "Murph Men." If I did it that way though, I'd be stuck in an endless cycle of internal conflict and heartbreak. The same is true of your financial behavior. You can take advice from the so-called experts on TV or follow stock tips from friends for the rest of your days, but until you look inside, and recognize whatever is driving your financial desires and decisions, and choose to overcome those forces, you'll remain trapped in survival mode.

The Financial Healing Process

I can't overstate the importance of these three steps:

1. *Examine your current cash flow and begin to make small changes in it, based on your personal goals.*

2. *Understand your patterns of financial behavior and their underlying causes.*

3. *Finally, have the courage to face the deep-rooted emotions behind those behaviors, and change your response to the discomfort they cause.*

This is how to live a financial life pointed toward achieving your dreams.

CHAPTER WRAP-UP

Transforming your current life into the one you truly desire doesn't happen overnight. You progress through the process in digestible, bite-size pieces.

Financial healing occurs both internally with your emotions, and externally in your day-to-day behavior.

You can begin to reshape your behavior by redirecting your cash flow, and by utilizing the power of intent.

When you give your money a specific purpose in short-term, mid-term and long-term timeframes according to your heart's desires, you are empowering it to manifest your dreams.

The internal healing process occurs once you come to terms with your innermost fears, disappointments, anxieties and discomforts. You must learn to process those feelings differently, rather than acting out in the form of unhealthy financial behavior, such as overspending.

*"Abundance is not something we acquire.
It is something we tune into."*

—Wayne Dyer

9

LIVES THAT THRIVE

I believe the best way for you to understand financial healing is to see how others have integrated their Inner Wealth into their financial lives. As you now know, I look at wealth building through a different lens than most of the people in my profession. For one thing, I don't believe in using demographics or age as guidelines for building a portfolio. There is no denying, however, that we all pass through different financial phases of life: Early Accumulation, Later Accumulation and Distribution. I use these descriptions of phases to help my clients ask themselves the right questions about their finances. Since examples are such wonderful teachers, I've chosen three client snapshots for us to look at. Here you will see how others have begun to achieve their life's hopes and dreams by altering how money flows through their lives.

Nick and Katrina

I first met Nick when he was a single guy in his mid-twenties. He had a full social calendar and a mountain of debt. Although he was described to me as a less than ideal client at the time, I felt he had a lot of potential for success. Nick worked in sales for a midsize manufacturer. The friend who referred him agreed that, despite his affinity for spending, Nick would probably be running the company someday.

A gregarious, fun-loving guy, Nick was the one who always picked up the tab at the end of the night, even if he was buying for strangers. After our first meeting, a few things became quite clear. Nick came from money, as many of my young clients do. He was smart and ambitious and knew how to make a buck, but nobody had ever taught him how to manage the flow of money. Throughout his life, his parents paid for everything; even his college tuition was paid in cash. Now he'd been out of school for five years and was making a pretty nice salary. But, as he put it, "Every month, I just piss it all away." Nick admitted that he really wanted to get a handle on his spending, but he didn't know where to start. In his initial consultation, he mentioned that he wanted his girlfriend, who was his childhood sweetheart, to be part of our planning sessions. Since there was talk of tying the knot, I suggested they both come in and go through the Life Navigation Wheel exercise together.

Katrina was also in her mid-twenties. A kind, warm-hearted soul, she worked as a nurse for a major hospital in Chicago. Her background was less affluent than Nick's. Because she had to earn her way through adolescence and college, she became, as an adult, quite adept at managing the flow of money. She knew how to stretch a dollar! Katrina was pleased with Nick's newfound interest in financial planning and was eager to join him in mapping out a future together. After going through the wheel exercise with them, I immediately saw a clear path to abundance for this promising young couple. Here are some of the highlights from our discovery session.

Financial

I had suspicions that Nick felt overwhelmed and a little shameful about his debt. My instincts were right. As he spoke about his financial status, he couldn't get over the fact that he'd let his spending get so out of control. Nick couldn't even see that he was drawing a healthy salary. In his mind, that debt overshadowed everything.

Katrina's financial state was also no surprise to me. Because of her upbringing, she had quite a bit of short-term cash on hand. An astute saver, she monitored every penny in her savings and checking accounts. During our meeting, Katrina expressed concern over Nick's debt. She revealed that it caused her a great deal of inner turmoil. To her, debt was a red warning flag that signaled financial failure on the horizon. Her immediate desire was to get married and purchase a home in a family-friendly community. She viewed Nick's debt as a roadblock to that dream. This realization eventually helped the two of them face their future with a great deal of mutual respect and understanding.

Career

Nick confided that he really wanted to be successful like his dad, and didn't know how he could get ahead in his current company. He liked his sales job but it lacked the mental stimulation he craved as a hungry young upstart. After a little soul-searching, he realized that in his heart he wanted to leave his present employer and return to his hometown to work for the company of his dreams.

Katrina truly enjoyed her nursing career. It provided a source of personal fulfillment and purpose. She also appreciated the flexibility that her profession allowed. This would come in handy later when little ones entered the picture.

Family

Both Nick and Katrina were eager to plan their wedding. Okay, I have to admit, Katrina was a bit more excited. They shared a mutual vision of the ceremony, location and number of guests. The ring was another story. She kept insisting that it didn't have to be extravagant or expensive. Nick just gave me a wink and said, "The ring is the only one I'll ever buy her, no replacements, so it better be a good one!" Also, because of her nurturing spirit, Katrina was eager to start a family, but she was not excited about raising children in Chicago. She longed to be near her parents and siblings back east.

Personal

At the time, Nick was traveling a lot for work. He stated that he actually enjoyed it. Although he'd been through practically every major airport in North America, he had never been to Mexico. A week of fun and adventure with the guys before the wedding was on his mind.

Katrina was thinking more long-term. She said that she had always wanted to join a health club. True to her profession, she looked at it as an investment in her health and well-being. Still, she felt there wasn't any extra money in her cash flow to cover the monthly fee.

Nick and Katrina's Plan

Armed with these and other insights, we went to work. Our first plan of attack was to get a handle on that debt. I've found that if you lock into a debt reduction plan and let it run on autopilot, your mind is free to focus on earning. This is precisely what we did. We put Nick on an offensive and defensive game plan. I explained that it isn't enough just to pay down the debt balance. That's just playing defense and no game is won by only playing one side of the game. You have to get offensive by socking money away in your short term bucket for other intentions.

The plan was for Nick was to allocate $600 a month to the credit card company and he was to put $50 each into his short-term, mid-term and long-term buckets. His company didn't offer a 401(k) plan, so we opened a Roth IRA for Nick's retirement, and a growth mutual fund to meet his mid-term needs. Every time he got a raise or bonus, he agreed to take the difference between his regular paycheck and the new amount and split it up. One third would go toward his debt; one third would go to increasing his lifestyle; the final third would be directed to building his wealth in all three buckets. It took him about three years to flatten the mountain of debt, but when he was done, he had also accumulated close to $10,000 in cash, which had been growing in an electronic savings account he named "Emergency Fund." He had two additional accounts that also served their purposes quite well: the "Ring Fund" and "House Fund."

I suggested that until the two married, they keep their money separate. Their individual contributions to the marital assets would bring positive energy to the relationship. My immediate plan for Katrina was to heavy up on her mid- and long-term savings. Although her employer offered a 403(b) plan, which is similar to a 401(k) but for not-for-profit companies, she chose to not enroll because there was no free money match from the hospital. We opened a Roth IRA for her long-term bucket and a low-risk mutual fund for her midterm needs. We chose the low-risk fund because of Katrina's sensitivity to significant swings in her balances. We were also able to get her that health club membership she'd been thinking about. First we lowered the cost of her auto insurance by raising the deductible. Then we decreased the number of exemptions on her W-2. These two actions freed up just enough monthly cash to afford her membership to one of the city's finest health clubs. The two were on their way to achieving their dreams.

To pay for the wedding, they took the money that Nick was no longer paying on his debt, along with other money from their cash flow, and socked it away in yet another online savings account. When the big day came, their parents paid for about half of the wedding costs, and Nick and Katrina paid for the other half in cash. There's something to be said about getting cash gifts at your wedding and not having to use them to pay off your wedding bill. The happy couple started their marriage in the black.

After the wedding, Nick and Katrina merged their short-term monies but left their other buckets separate. This is a personal choice that every couple should make consciously. There is no right or wrong, just whatever makes both parties comfortable. A couple of months after the wedding, Nick applied for his dream job back in their hometown on the East Coast. When he was offered the position, they had already made their moving plans. Because of their diligence in sticking to our plan, they were able to make a hefty down payment on a new home in a family-oriented neighborhood. Katrina took a nursing job at the community hospital and was even able to transfer her health club membership to a sister facility. By the time they had their first child, four-and-a-half years after our first meeting, Nick was socking away $2,700 a month total in all three buckets. This is the same guy who could barely save $150 a month when we met! All we did was use new money to create more money. Because Nick went after his desire to leave Chicago and work for a different company, now he not only loves his job, he enjoys a more balanced, harmonious life. He stopped focusing on the money and the debt and went after what he wanted—an inspiring career, a beautiful wife and a family of their own.

Some Adjustments

I've been working with Nick and Katrina for many years now. We get together semi-annually to revisit the Life Navigation Wheel and adjust their portfolio accordingly. In our most recent meeting, we discussed saving for their child's college years, since both Katrina and Nick want to pay for 100% of their son's tuition. This will be easy, since they simply shifted their savings into a College Fund instead of searching for things to sacrifice to help their child. Katrina is now thinking about writing children's books, so we put money aside to help her develop her talent. Their friends look at them and ask, "How are you doing this?" The answer is easy. It's because they made a choice to change their financial future.

This couple's story is not unusual. But it's theirs to tell, and that's what makes it special. Nick and Katrina are an example of a family in the early accumulation years. They are focused on their dreams of providing a safe, loving environment as well as a life of abundance for their children. I am certain they will continue to look inward as they progress together in their life journey.

Jack and Diane

I have their daughter, Maggie, to thank for introducing me to Jack and Diane. I was in my second year as an independent planner when Maggie, who's my friend from business school, called, insistent that I work with her parents. Apparently word of my approach to wealth management had made its way back to her. A few days later Maggie's mom called.

Within a week, I found myself sitting across from quite an astounding couple. Jack and Diane were the poster children for the sandwich generation (a boomer couple caring for their kids and aging parents). These hard-working fifty-somethings had just finished putting one daughter, Maggie, through college. The second child, also a girl, had two years left at her father's Big Ten alma mater, which meant that they were on the cusp of getting the biggest pay raise of their lives, since they would have no more college expenses. Up until the previous year, both of their mothers had been alive and in need of long-term care. They lovingly supported their moms physically, financially and emotionally, throughout the rest of their lives.

Here's the part that really makes this couple remarkable. Jack, a mechanical engineer, and Diane, a hospital administrator, celebrated their empty nest years by going back to school to earn their MBAs! At the time of our first meeting, each of them had just reached senior management positions in their respective fields. Because they had been a double-income couple throughout their entire marriage, they were able to pay cash for their daughters' tuitions and fund their graduate degrees while amassing quite a sizeable nest egg for themselves.

At this point you may be wondering why a successful couple like Jack and Diane would need help from a financial professional. They seemed to be doing pretty well on their own. Here's a fact that you may have overlooked. Once the children are out of school and the house is paid for, you no longer have tuition credits or mortgage interest write-offs on your taxes. This means no more dependents to claim (unless the kids boomerang back, which is an emerging trend these days), and no more deductions for retirement savings once your 401(k)s and IRAs are maxed out. Are you getting the picture?

Our walk through the Life Navigation Wheel was fascinating, to say the least. This dynamic duo, who appeared to have achieved every one of their life goals, sat there like two lumps on a log when faced with the question, "What's next?"

Personal

After the first few cricket-chirping minutes of silence, it was plain to see that these folks desperately needed a new purpose in life. This is a natural state that occurs in boomer parents. By the time the kids are out of the house, they've spent a lifetime providing for and taking care of others. Suddenly they're forced to consider, "What do we want out of life?" It's a seemingly unanswerable question to those who have just exhausted twenty years fulfilling parental obligations, followed closely by a season of caring for their own beloved moms and dads.

Diane finally broke the silence. "I've always wanted to sail to Belize," she offered timidly. Go, Diane, go! Before long, she was picturing them aboard a sailboat charter from Miami.

It didn't take Jack long to get onboard. In addition to sailing, his passion was electronics, and I don't mean collecting them. He was quite adept at assembling hard drives and motherboards to create his own PCs. Wouldn't it be great if he could start up a sort of computer boutique where he could sell his cyber creations, he wondered. He also admitted that he secretly had his eye on a second Harley Davidson. They were finally getting the hang of dreaming, and finding out what their desires really were.

Family

The conversation quickly turned to weddings and grandchildren. Clearly, this realm of the wheel was easy for them to explore. They felt pretty confident that their two girls were the marrying kind and would need some wedding subsidization in the next few years. They shared a desire to provide up to 75% of the funds for whatever type of soiree the girls dreamed of. They also shared a desire to create a college fund for any grandkids that might arrive in the not-so-distant future. They also needed to couple this with caring for their aging mothers.

Career

Diane really felt passionate about her career. She loved her work enough to be successful, but respected her marriage enough to leave the office at five o'clock most days. Her dream was to remain committed to her career for another five years. After that, she wanted to work with the hospital staff on a consulting basis—that is, whenever she wasn't sailing to the coast of Central America. Jack was a hard worker, but he had already spent some time searching for his passion. He had changed jobs four times in twelve years. As a result, he had a string of 401(k) funds in various investment firms. He shared his dream of building custom computers and selling them from his basement workshop, a thought that brought a wide grin to his otherwise imperturbable expression.

Financial

Despite the seven-hundred-and-fifty thousand dollar nest egg in their collective retirement accounts, their financial future was a source of angst for both Jack and Diane. He had already maxed out his 401(k) along with an after-tax IRA. The upcoming loss in tax deductions weighed heavily on them. They really wanted some peace of mind for the future. Like most boomers I know, they were living in the same modest house they had purchased twenty years ago. The mortgage was three years away from being paid off, and they no longer were getting a tax break on the interest, since they were just paying on the principal. The house was in good shape. It just needed the usual repairs and maintenance, something that they had always paid for with cash. Jack had kept his $30,000 inheritance from his mother sitting in a low-interest savings account. He shared that he was unsure what to do with the money. Because it was his mother's money, it had emotional significance. He couldn't put it just anywhere.

I felt that our first task together was to address the balances in their buckets or lack thereof. This would help us get a handle on how to fund their well-earned dreams of freedom and independence. Because they both worked, they really didn't have time to spend a lot of money. This allowed them the luxury of paying cash for their graduate degrees and their daughters' college tuitions. Although their long-term and short-term funds were quite ample, they had no mid-term money to speak of. It was time for Jack and Diane to direct the cash flow to each of their three buckets on a monthly basis. I suggested that they explore real estate limited partnerships as a mid-term investment. This would give them some additional tax breaks, for example only having to pay 15% in capital gains tax. Plus, they would avoid being taxed in their ordinary income tax bracket of 35%. It would also provide them with an additional source of income for short-term contingencies. They certainly didn't need thirty grand in their short-term bucket, but they did need enough to cover a new roof and the future wedding days they hoped would arrive. With Jack's agreement, we took half of his inheritance and opened five online savings accounts: one named "Emergency Reserves," one named "Belize," one named "Wedding," another named "House Repairs" and the fifth one, "Harley." They eagerly promised to deposit a small percentage of their monthly income in each account. Something to note here is that, like all couples, their desires changed over time. A few years later, while revisiting their dreams for the future, Diane decided that she also wanted a Harley. So we opened an additional account earmarked "Motorcycle Mama." Lucky for me, most of my clients have a sense of humor when it comes to naming their savings accounts. Money can be very dry, so do make it fun whenever you can!

Easing Their Transition

Jack and Diane are examples of people transitioning from accumulation to distribution years. Although a bit dubious at first, about what they wanted out of life for themselves, the two settled in nicely with their new plan. The last time we met, Jack had already built three computers and sold one. He was ecstatic.

I'd like to put in an aside here for parents with children headed for college. If you have chosen to let them take out student loans, you should consider what will happen if they default on one of those loans. I've seen it happen to the best of them—great kids, smart kids who, for whatever reason, stop making payments after about a year out of school. Well, the government is getting wise to this, and now parents are required to cosign on their children's student loan, regardless of their financial state. Unless you create a game plan in case this unfortunate event becomes a reality, guess who's left holding the bag?

Carl and Ann

Carl came to me when he was in his late fifties. A software engineer for a big West Coast company, he had a good track record saving and spending. Luckily for the both of them, he knew how to make money and hold onto it. Then, one year after he became my client, he was unexpectedly downsized out of his job, a position he'd held for twenty-nine years. It seemed retirement was coming sooner than he had expected.

There's something you should know about folks who are forced into an early retirement. They're traumatized. I find this especially true of men in their late fifties to early sixties. Suddenly, they're wondering what the next thirty years of their lives are going to be like. Their parents lived in a time when life expectancy was shorter, investments weren't readily available, and earning a living wasn't always easy. That generation didn't have many years left after they retired. Today's average retiree has roughly a third of his or her life left to enjoy and, I'm sorry to say, ambiguity to face about the long-term reliability of Social Security and Medicare benefits.

The dynamic between Carl and Ann was interesting. Ann never worked outside the home, except for some part-time volunteer work. A lovely, quiet woman, she devoted her life to raising their sons and supporting her husband in his demanding career. When we first met, she let Carl do most of the talking. Money was his domain. But I could tell by the way she looked at him and the few comments she made that she probably knew her husband better than he knew himself. They were soul mates and very much in love.

Their initial journey through the four circles of the wheel was almost as difficult for them as it was for Jack and Diane. People really find learning how to dream challenging these days.

Finance

Carl was the kind of guy who did everything right. His money management skills were no exception. The couple lived in a popular suburb outside Chicago. The modest home they had purchased twenty-five years before was now worth about half a million dollars. A novice landscape architect, Carl had spent the last fifteen years turning their grassy suburban lot into a woodland oasis. Ann had quite an eye for décor. Their home was picture-perfect, inside and out. As much as they loved their place, the couple agreed that someday they'd be ready to leave. Little did we know that that move would take place much earlier than expected! Carl mentioned Florida as a dream spot for the new home, while Ann suggested San Diego, since their sons lived there with their families. I got the feeling that was the first time she'd ever spoken up for what she really wanted.

Career

In our initial meeting, Carl reported that he enjoyed going to work every day. He couldn't imagine what else he'd ever want to do for mental stimulation. Ann suggested that perhaps he might like to take a part-time job at a garden center someday. Carl nodded, but he didn't seem enthused by the idea.

Family

With grown children in their thirties and two grandchildren, Carl and Ann had mixed feelings about leaving the Midwest. Family was important to them, almost more than their independence. As we discussed their options, I pointed out that if they didn't move to California, they could keep a travel fund available for frequent visits with their sons and their families. Carl's mother was in her late eighties at the time and still lived on her own in a nearby apartment. He couldn't fathom leaving her or moving her to a senior care facility. He had grown up the oldest child of five. His father worked long hours to put food on the table. Carl and his mom were very close. Naturally, he felt it was his duty to care for her in her later years. I thought it interesting that he had re-created the exact life he had as a child, career dad, stay-at-home mom and numerous children—again, a perfect example of re-creating the familiar!

Personal

Since Ann had nursed both parents through old age, and Carl was still caring for his mom, they were very open to discussing their own future need for long-term care. The couple agreed that they did not want their children burdened by their health or housing needs. The picture they painted for their future had them funding their own private health care, and eventually living together in an upscale retirement community.

At our first meeting, Carl still had his job. Consequently, our initial strategy was to stabilize their buckets and build up their mid-term money. Due to Carl's Midas touch, their finances were in pretty good shape. He had a reasonable balance in savings and checking accounts for short-term needs. At the time, all he had for the next three to five years were a few savings bonds. Remember, mutual funds didn't come into wide use by the middle class until the mid '80s, so for the first half of his career, bonds were a popular and safe investment. His long-term money was spread out in a variety of pension funds and 401(k)s. Again, employer retirement plans like 401(k)s weren't around before the Reagan era. Employees relied on pensions to save for their golden years. We consolidated his retirement money into one IRA, and began devising a plan to save for private health care. Then the news broke about Carl's layoff.

That event understandably hit Carl right between the eyes. His whole life's purpose was obliterated and, sadly, not by choice. Stunned, he called me to set up an emergency planning session to ensure their security. He admitted to me on the phone that it would take some time to recoup his ego and find a new source of stimulation.

The first decision he made was to sell the house and move to San Diego. He happily honored his wife's desire to be close to their sons and agreed to move west. With the sizeable lump sum they received from the sale of their home, they were able to purchase a lovely place and also secure a condo for his mother in a senior community close by. They settled in and lived quite comfortably with their money on autopilot. Carl even took a part-time job in the home and garden department of a large home improvement chain store.

For a man like Carl, it wasn't surprising that the emotional impact of his job loss eventually took its toll. His entire self-image was wrapped up in his role as provider. With this taken away, he felt vulnerable and lost. This is a perfect example of what can happen when we let toxic emotions build up inside. Over time they took up residence in his first chakra zone (the foundation of his identity) and wreaked havoc on his health. Fifteen months after his termination, Carl was diagnosed with colon cancer. The good news is that because we planned for ample health care with his retirement money, he was able to receive cutting-edge treatment and eventually became cancer-free. Although it's not my place to recommend medical treatment, my hope was that Carl would seek counsel from a therapist or psychologist to heal the wounds of having been jolted out of something he considered to be his life's purpose.

CHAPTER WRAP-UP

Every couple should consciously decide how they want to merge their money when they marry. There is no right or wrong, just what makes both parties comfortable.

When people in the "sandwich generation" pass the twin obligations of college tuition and caring for their parents, they will lose some tax advantages.

It's often hard for people facing retirement to learn how to dream again.

If forced into early retirement, it makes sense to seek out your soul's purpose from this point forward.

"Start by doing what's necessary; then do what's possible; and suddenly you are doing the impossible."

—Saint Francis of Assisi

10

BUILDING AND RENOVATING YOUR PORTFOLIO

Your investment portfolio, along with your plan for protecting your assets and building wealth, should be an organic, ever-evolving navigational map. It bears repeating that this should not be the static, one-size-fits-all list of products that many professionals would have you rely on. Your life will progress through many changes from the time you start accumulating wealth to the time that you're ready to live off the fruits of your labor. Dreams change, goals change, even the products you choose can change. CDs are a good example of what I'm talking about. Chances are that if you purchased a CD in the '80s, you were offered a higher interest rate for opening it. Today, those same CDs are probably earning less. Stocks are another good example. Most people who inherit stocks don't sell them because they think they are still serving the same purpose that they were initially—to earn income. However, those stocks may no longer be performing as well as they were when your loved one purchased them. It pays to do a little research.

Ask Your Advisor to Please Speak in Plain English

How many times have you been listening to your banker, stockbroker, or even your favorite insurance salesperson explain one of their products, and your eyes start to glaze over? It isn't long before they sound like Charlie Brown's teacher—bwah, bwah, bwah, bwah, bwah! Every time I say this to a client, he or she says, "Yeah, you're right!" That's because my industry is filled with left-brainers.

Their minds function predominantly in the realms of logic, analysis and rational thought. Today's typical financial services professional looks at banking, risk management and investing as a black-and-white logical discipline. Most newbie brokers fresh out of college are whip-smart, you can bet on that, but most of them tend to look at you and your needs solely from a logical and rational point of view. So do the guys with the big corner offices who hire them. They think in terms of statistics and technical or fundamental investment analysis. That's what makes them good at understanding money to begin with.

The majority of financial services clients are not analytically focused, or else they would be managing their financial portfolios themselves. They're generally right-brain thinkers who tend to look at life more holistically, subjectively, and yes, emotionally. Let me just say here that we all use both sides of our brains, and that having a dominant right or left is neither right nor wrong. However, the dynamics that currently exist between financial professionals and their clients is often a misalignment. There's an apparent disconnect between the industry as a whole and the individuals it serves. On the one hand, you have an intelligent, analytical, objective financial salesperson spewing out Alpha, Beta and Sharpe ratios, which sound pretty much like alphabet soup to most consumers (and it's okay to understand as much or as little as you'd like). On the other side of the desk, you have clients who are more inclined to think intuitively or subjectively when it comes to money. So those clients are looking at their brokers, saying, "Huh?"

Because They Told Me To

I can't tell you how many clients have come to me at totally different stages of life, and with completely different personalities and attitudes about money, all saying the same thing. When I ask them why they bought into this fund or that plan, without fail everyone gives me the same answer: "Because this is the product they told me to buy." Let me tell you, my friend, based on what I now understand about emotions and money, this is just plain wrong! You should not have anything in your investment or insurance portfolio because somebody else said so, or even worse, because it made someone else wealthier. You need to make sure that the products you purchase are first and foremost in alignment with your personal strategy. Make it all about you, not them! If you do that, it will be much easier to remember the reason you're getting that product in the first place.

Creating Your Investment and Risk Management Portfolio

Let's look at the pyramid below called "Client Advocacy Relationship." As you see, it's divided into three horizontal sections. The section at bottom or base of the pyramid is "Personal Strategy." The middle section is "Personal Portfolio," containing the types of investments and insurance that comprise your portfolio. The top section is "Products," which represents the vast amounts of choices in the marketplace you have that can compliment your current reality. This diagram illustrates my approach to creating an abundant future. You begin the process by creating a strategy based on you as an individual, you and your spouse, or your immediate family. Next, you analyze your portfolio and compare it to your current personal or household strategy. The last step is to select the financial products that are best suited to align your goals and aspirations to your financial product choices, products that complement or replace those in the current portfolio you already have in place.

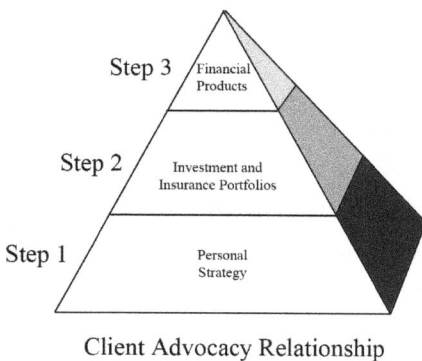

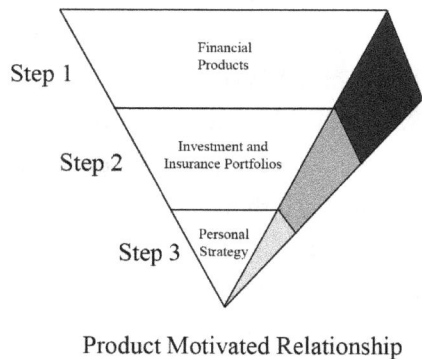

Client Advocacy Relationship

Product Motivated Relationship

Interestingly, many financial services professionals have this backwards. They start the process with the products they have to offer. This is called a "Product Driven Relationship." Then they determine where those products fit into your portfolio. Lastly, they create a strategy for you based on how you can use their products. Not only is this limiting for you, it has the wrong motivation behind it. It would be the same as going to your favorite department store and having to buy a flaming red, size 18 dress even though you're really a size 8 and look fabulous in navy blue. But you have no choice, because big red dresses are the only thing that they have on the rack. Does this kind of shopping make sense to you?

You absolutely cannot build a foundation for financial success when you start with a product, let alone a limited selection of products. You build wealth by choosing your personal strategy, then looking at the investments and insurance that you already have, and determining if they support your personal strategy and are right for you. In the end, you should choose from the entire world of products to implement the rest of your personal strategy, and get it all in the right alignment.

Again, everything should start with you. The day my industry begins thinking this way is the day there will be a massive shift in power from them to you. It will be the dawn of an entirely new era in financial planning and wealth management, and a beautiful dawn at that.

Financial Makeover

When talking about investment portfolios and insurance products, I love to use the analogy of a closet full of clothes. Most people have a whole lot of random "financial clothes" in their closets, but nothing is coordinated into outfits. Your job now is to clean out your closet, get rid of the stuff that's out-of-date and create a smart new collection of ensembles according to your own personality and tastes. This will prepare you for your first meeting with that new financial professional who is ready to be your quarterback. It will also give you a little more insight into the person behind those purchases… you!

21　EXERCISE

Portfolio Exercise

So what's in your portfolio? It's time for you to get in there, take it apart and see. Go through all of your folders, statements, policies, etc. Take a piece of paper and make three columns. Label them Short-Term, Mid-Term and Long-Term. Now go through your investments and insurance policies and try to put them in their respective buckets. Even if you don't know why you have that term life insurance, or aren't sure where it goes, take your best guess. Remember, it's all tied to timelines. Everyone has a different threshold when it comes to understanding finances and financial products. You may instinctively know which products belong in which bucket, or you may not have a clue. You should take a look at the products in your portfolio and try to make sense of them to the level that you're comfortable with. Do the best you can.

The Importance of Diversification

Before we go any further, I want to say something about diversification. As mentioned earlier, it has been proven by Ibbotson Associates that approximately 92% of your investment performance is based on how well you diversify your assets. This is the foundation of "modern portfolio theory," or MPT as we call it in the biz. In plain English, this simply means spreading yourself out. Let's say that, heaven forbid, one of the firms you've invested in decides to change ownership and, because of a poorly managed transition, goes under. If you only have 5% of your money in that company, that's not going to hit you as hard as it would if you had 50% in it. That would be devastating. I'm not saying that losing 5% wouldn't sting. Sure it would, but you could get up the next day and move on. One of the worst mistakes I see people make is not diversifying their assets, almost always for emotional reasons.

Who's Leading Your Team?

For the purposes of this book, I am going to assume that you're not someone who wants to go it alone, meaning you do not choose to invest the time or emotion in building or revising your own financial plan. If you have the confidence—and time—for that, bless you (and feel free to contact me at www. EmotionBehindMoney.com if you ever find yourself lost in a sea of confusing options and prospectuses). For most people, finding the right partner or client advocate to help you achieve your dreams is essential to your success and happiness. I suggest you approach it as you would to find anyone where trust is key. Meet a lot of people, ask a lot of questions and get references! You're looking for a very significant person in your life, and you don't want to settle for just anyone. Also in my opinion, you want a financial planner who is fee-based, not commission-based. This way you have someone who is truly on your team. The more money you make, the more money your advisor makes, whether he or she is called a broker, planner, advisor or vice president. The more you lose, the more they lose. If your advisor has the same incentive you have to make sure you succeed in your financial goals, you'll both be on the same playing field.

The Client Advocate

Fee-based advisors are likely to be compensated to support a client advocacy relationship. They are paid by a company, bank or investment firm that promotes ongoing service. As such they are highly motivated financially to be your advocate. Let me say this again, a financial professional cannot help you achieve wealth and abundance unless he or she understands the underlying cause of your current situation, your emotion behind money, and is able to shift your funds to your best advantage. Otherwise, that person can end up being another crab in your bucket, not a facilitator on your journey to true happiness.

Here are some questions to ask while shopping for financial professionals, independent or otherwise:

✓ Is your income fee-based or commission-based?

✓ What designations do you have? (I suggest looking for a Certified Financial Planner or CFP®).

✓ Are you tied to any sales goals with specific products?

✓ Are you working with any vendors who require you to sell a minimum number of their products or your contract with them will end? (Do you have any quotas to reach?)

✓ What are your limitations, if any, in selling specific product lines due to your current licensing? (Someone who is fully licensed has a Series 7 and Series 66 to be fee-based.)

✓ Do you charge an annual planning fee outside of compensation from products? If you don't, why not?

✓ If you're talking to an independent planner: If something were to happen to you, who will take care of me?

✓ If you're talking to someone associated with a firm: What happens if you leave the business, by choice, disability or death? Who would then be managing my money?

Your Financial Quarterback

I love football. When I was growing up, if we weren't watching a Chicago Bears or Notre Dame game on TV, we were rooting for one of the youth teams in the neighborhood. Is it any wonder I married a man who coaches football? My favorite position is quarterback. It requires brains, brawn and heart. These are also the qualifications you should be looking for in a financial professional. As you step into the game of building wealth, you need your own quarterback, someone who has your best interests at heart.

Your financial quarterback should possess the following qualities:

- Empathy

- Passion

- Conviction

- Tough Love

- Clarity

As I've said before, most wealth management professionals never get to the underlying causes of your financial behavior. To continue the football metaphor, they work from the sidelines, more like a player's agent, working on commission. You don't want somebody to be your agent; you want someone who is out on the field with you. You want a professional who keeps his eyes on your life goals instead of a big commission!

There is a huge disconnect between my industry and the public. For many years, financial products have been and still are being sold for all the wrong reasons, and those reasons have little to do with who you are as an individual. Recently, an audience member approached me after one of my seminars. He confided that he felt overwhelmed by the number of financial products made available to him by his stable of financial vendors. He knew that, at the end of the day, he was the only decision maker. This made him feel uneasy. He felt unqualified to put all of the disparate pieces together. What was he to base his decisions on? He felt he had an enormous orchestra playing all around him; yet there was no conductor to create harmony out of the chaos. I explained to him that this is the value of a fee-based financial planner. Because he needed tax, estate and retirement planning, plus a myriad of strategies that create wealth and abundance, a CFP was the best professional for him because only a fee-based advisor will be compensated in such a way that allows him or her to take time to explore the clients' personality and emotions, in addition to that clients' current financial reality. I strongly recommend that you, dear reader, also seek out someone to play that role for you. To do otherwise may pay off with luck, but it's certainly not setting yourself up to be lucky.

Get Rid of Belittling Advisors

I've met many clients who come to me for help, but at first feel reluctant to share their financial history with me. Inevitably, it turns out that their previous financial professionals made them feel ashamed of themselves. They were led to believe that they could only have low expectations because they "should have done this earlier" or "shouldn't have done that at all." "Tsk tsk, we'll try to make the best of a bad situation," they say. Yet, whenever we want to create a new reality, we have to take a good look at where we are without judgment. That desire to go after your dreams has got to be greater than the fears that you're not good enough. If you give into these toxic emotions, fear and shame will keep you where you are and prevent you from achieving long-lasting change.

The last thing you need is a belittling advisor. But there is good help available. You do not have to go it alone. We all need supports around us, and I like to think of mine as pillars. That's what you want your financial advisor to be. If you have a financial professional in your life who makes you feel bad about yourself, or pooh-poohs your dreams, stop trying to explain yourself, pick up your money, and move on. Seek out friends and acquaintances who rave about their financial professional. Get that wealth advisor's number and give the person a call. Look for someone who really listens to you, and helps you make the plans to seek your heart's desires.

A Personal "Board of Directors"

In addition to finding a financial professional to lead you to victory, it's helpful to create your own personal board of directors. Make a list of people who know you and have your best interests at heart. Choose friends or professional mentors, anyone who isn't afraid to tell it like it is, should you fall back into unhealthy patterns of behavior. For example, if you should get an uncontrollable urge to go out on a spending bender, you'll have someone to call who will help you stay tethered to your goals. These should be people you admire, and who you give permission to say, "Don't do that. It will keep you from getting where you want to be, my friend." It must be people who don't make you feel ashamed, or it won't work. Think of them as lighthouses. When storms come rolling in, as storms always will, you'll have them as beams of light to lead you to safety. Also, don't forget to say "Thank you. More please." Gratitude expressed to the Universe (and of course to people as well) goes a long way.

I've always said that despite the tough times when I was the kid with eleven siblings, we always, no matter what, had each other. I've always known that I will never, ever hit rock bottom, because my loved ones will pull me up if I fall. You can have a similar supportive atmosphere surrounding you every day. You build it by being the kind of friend you want to have. And (see above) don't forget to express your gratitude to all those who help you along the way. It will fuel the cycle of friendship and good fortune for the rest of your life!

CHAPTER WRAP-UP

Financial folks are typically left-brain thinkers. They speak in a language that is rooted in analytics and logic. The typical financial services client is more right-brain dominant. They function in a world that is more intuitive and creative. This has created a huge disconnect between the industry and the people it serves.

The contents of your portfolio should be aligned with the person you have come to know a little better throughout this book—you!

Your portfolio should be created in accordance with who you are as an individual, rather than accepting the products that a financial advisor offers.

Before you can create a portfolio exclusively around your true self, it's helpful to become acquainted with the financial products you currently own.

You don't have to fully understand each product. Learn about them to the extent you feel comfortable.

Seek a financial advisor who embraces your individuality. Look for a financial quarterback, an advocate, someone who will be out there on the field with you, rather than on the sidelines.

Surround yourself with a personal "board of directors"—mentors, close friends and family members who can support you as you replace unhealthy financial behaviors with healthier ones.

"Success in life could be defined as the continued expansion of happiness and the progressive realization of worthy goals. Success is the ability to fulfill your desires with effortless ease. And yet success, including the creation of wealth, has always been considered to be a process that requires hard work and it is often considered to be at the expense of others. We need a more spiritual approach to success and to affluence which is the abundant flow of all good things to you."

—Deepak Chopra

EPILOGUE
WELCOME TO THE BEGINNING

The process in this book marks a new trend in the financial industry. It's time to put the futility of survival mode behind us. It's time for you to thrive! To be honest, the process itself never really ends. It should continue throughout your life. In a year, you may decide that you don't want that big house after all, that it's more important for you to travel. Or maybe you want an even bigger house because your desire now is to adopt a dozen underprivileged children. If that's the case, adjust the money flowing through your buckets accordingly. Love yourself enough to continue dreaming. Who cares how many times you change your mind; it's your life! Just remember, your reality is what you have created, not anyone else.

Monitoring and measuring are two activities to embrace throughout the life of any financial plan. Monitor your desires and measure your growth. If an investment isn't pulling in the numbers you need to reach your goal, change it. Understand that there will be times of expansion and contraction. The financial markets breathe just like a human being. There will be times of growth and times of reduction. It's the overall timeframe you must focus on. Consider your timeframes or buckets before making any drastic changes. Here's what I tell every client as they move forward from this point:

1. Feel empowered and energetic about the process.

2. Live as if you have already achieved your dreams and desires.

3. Surround yourself with a support team.

4. Be positive.

5. Wish the "crabs in your bucket" well, and move on.

6. Tell yourself new stories of success, not failures.

7. Lead by example—transform yourself and others will follow.

Other Resources

As far as tracking your progress, my advice is to understand as much as you want to, to the extent you want to. There's so much information available today that it can be paralyzing if you're not careful. There are companies that generate market reports that are easy to understand. It doesn't always have to be daunting. Whatever you do, though, don't take your financials and stick them under the mattress, so to speak. Stay involved as best you can. Remember, it's not rocket science—it just sounds like it. Forbes, Fortune and Crain's, among other fine business publications, offer jargon-free reports and analyses for people who speak plain English.

Benediction

By now, you should be able to see how your finances and your life's purpose are woven tightly together by your intentions. My hope is that the collective exercises and processes in this book allowed you to hear what your inner voice is trying to tell you. Some people refer to that inner voice as the Holy Spirit; others call it the Universe; and still others believe it's their soul. You might just attribute it to that elusive right-brain asset we call intuition. Call it what you wish. The important thing is to listen to what it's saying. The answers are not always immediately clear, but just the fact that you're asking questions of your life opens your future to a myriad of exciting possibilities and positive change. We all want more out of life. We all want more than our reality currently offers. The key here is to define that "more" beyond the scope of money. Abundance isn't just money. It's also about unplugging from the social pressure to own a new car, a big house and a closet full of shoes, and instead tap into what you truly value—happiness, joy, hope, faith, honesty, love, compassion. No matter how many wealthy people I meet, the story seldom changes. You can earn it all and buy it all, but at the end of the day there's still that inner desire for something else. I believe that "something else" is your life's purpose or passion. Follow that, my friend, you will have it all, and the money will follow!

Thank you for taking this journey with me!

APPENDIX 1

If you were able to go to work every day and do what you'd be absolutely passionate about doing, day in and day out, what would that be?

List your "top five" passions below in no particular order.

1. _____
2. _____
3. _____
4. _____
5. _____

Public Relations

Finding Target Markets

Plans/Strategies

Package Products/Services

Financial Plans

Telemarketing

Working with Your Hands

Recruiting Key Personnel

Sales Management

Research

Identifying Prospects

Sales Processes

Analysis

Internet Maintenance

Asset Selection

Customer Relations

Asset Allocation

Managing Phone Systems

Arranging Quarterly Meetings

Training

Human Resources

Compter Systems

Educating

Creating Company Mission

Writing Proposals

Product/Service Development

Managing Key Personnel

Strategic Planning

Qualifying Prospects

Financial Performance Reports

Investment Policy

Client Services

Working with a Team

Maintenance Office Equipment

Multitasking

Sales Presentations

Opening Accounts

Re-Balancing Financials

Working at a Desk

Quarterly Financials

Client Welcome Packets

Client/Customer Correspondence

Creating Employee Files

Personnel Systems and Procedures

Employee Wellness

Networking

Charitable Work

Ad Placement

Employment Applications

Orgaizing

Job Training

Employee Manual

Connecting People

Big Ideas

Compliance

Relationship Building

Working Outside

Employee Recruiting

Database Maintenance

Employee Position Contracts

Inventing

Investing Strategies

Creating Presentations

Current Portfolio Analysis

Retirement Needs Analysis

Working with the Elderly

Job Candidate Approvals

Employee Background Checks

Lead Generation Systems

Strategic Thinking

Work with Children

Media Communications

Company Event Planning

Welcome Packets for Clients

Tax Reporting

General Facility Operations

Arranging

Warm Fuzzies

Meeting Goals

Finding Niche Markets

Business Structuring

Product Design/Specifications

Vendor Relations

Newsletters

APPENDIX 2

Suggested Reading and Other Resources

Personal Life:

Health:

Chopra, Deepak. *Perfect Health: The Complete Mind/Body Guide, Revised and Updated Edition*. New York: Three Rivers Press, 2001. www.chopra.com

Hay, Louise L. *You Can Heal Your Life*. Carlsbad, CA: Hay House, Inc., 1984.

Myss, Carolyn. *Anatomy of the Spirit: The Seven Stages of Power and Healing*. New York: Three Rivers Press, 1997. www.carolynmyss.com

Simon, David, M.D. *The Wisdom of Healing: A Natural Mind Body Program for Optimal Wellness*. New York: Three Rivers Press, 1998.

Chakras:

Chakra Illustration, www.myss.com/library/chakras/

Brennan, Barbara Ann. *Hands of Light: A Guide to Healing Through the Human Energy Field*. New York: Bantam Books, 1988.

_____. *Light Emerging: The Journey of Personal Healing*. New York: Bantam Books, 1993.

Personal Growth:

Byrne, Rhonda. *The Secret*. New York: Simon & Schuster Atria Books/Beyond Words, 2006.

Day, Laura. The Circle: *How the Power of a Single Wish Can Change Your Life*. New York: Jeremy P. Tarcher Putnam, 2001.

_____. *Welcome to Your Crisis: How to Use the Power of Crisis to Create the Life You Want.* New York: Little, Brown and Company, 2006.

Pettigrew, Karyn. *The Invitation: The Secret to Creating Your Best Life.* Chicago: Highest Good Publications, 2007.

Tolle, Eckhardt. *The Power of Now: A Guide to Spiritual Enlightenment.* Novato, CA: New World Library, 1999.

Inner Wealth/Spiritual Growth:
Chopra, Deepak. *Power, Freedom, and Grace: Living from the Source of Lasting Happiness.* Novato, CA: New World Library, Amber-Allen Publishing, 2006.

_____. *The Seven Spiritual Laws of Success: A Practical Guide to the Fulfillment of Your Dreams.* Novato, CA: New World Library, Amber-Allen Publishing, 1994.

Tolle, Eckhardt. *A New Earth: Awakening to Your Life's Purpose.* New York: Plume, a division of Penguin, 2008. www.eckharttolle.com

Williamson, Marianne. *Everyday Grace.* New York: Riverhead Books–Penguin Putnam, 2002. 2002. www.marianne.com

_____. *The Age of Miracles: Embracing the New Midlife.* Carlsbad, CA: Hay House, Inc., 2008.

Work Life:
Blanchard, Ken. *Gung Ho! Turn on the People in Any Organization.* New York: William Morrow, 1998.

Buford, Bob. *Halftime: Changing Your Game Plan from Success to Significance.* Grand Rapids, MI: Zondervan Publishing, 1994.

Collins, Jim. *Good to Great: Why Some Companies Make the Leap... and Others Don't.* New York : HarperCollins, 2001.

Gladwell, Malcolm. *The Tipping Point: How Little Things Can Make a Big Difference.* New York: Little, Brown and Company, 2000.

Kelly, Matthew. *The Dream Manager.* New York, Hyperion Books, 2007.

Pettigrew, Karyn. *I Quit, and Choose Work That Aligns with My Soul.* Chicago: KP Consulting, 2002.

Family Life:

The Dalai Lama and Howard C. Cutler. *The Art of Happiness: A Handbook for Living.* New York: Riverhead Books, 1998.

Engler, Scott Michael. *The Ten Secrets: A Short Tale of Redemption.* Tuttle, OK: SME Publishing Group, 2005.

Ruiz, Don Miguel. *The Four Agreements: A Practical Guide to Personal Freedom.* Novato, CA: New World Library, Amber-Allen Publishing, 2001.

www.ingramcontent.com/pod-product-compliance
Lightning Source LLC
Chambersburg PA
CBHW071557210326
41597CB00019B/3293